Critical Thinking About
Environmental Issues

Global
Warming

Critical Thinking About
Environmental Issues

Global
Warming

Other books in the Critical Thinking About
Environmental Issues series include:

Endangered Species
Pesticides

Critical Thinking About
Environmental Issues

Global Warming

by Jane S. Shaw

Senior Associate
PERC, the Center for Free
Market Environmentalism

**GREENHAVEN
PRESS ®**

San Diego • Detroit • New York • San Francisco • Cleveland
New Haven, Conn. • Waterville, Maine • London • Munich

LIBRARY OF CONGRESS CATALOGING-IN-PUBLICATION DATA

Global warming / by Jane S. Shaw, book editor.
    p. cm. — (Critical thinking about environmental issues series)
Summary: Discusses controversies surrounding global warming such as whether the
threat actually exists, how our climate is changing, what can be done to reduce the
greenhouse effect, and how our lives will change.
Includes bibliographical references and index.
ISBN 0-7377-1270-8 (hbk.)
  1. Global warming—Juvenile literature. [1. Global warming.] I. Shaw, Jane S., 1944–
II. Series.
  QC981.8.G56 G576 2002
  363.738'747—dc21

                                    2002001248

Printed in the United States of America

Contents

Foreword

If a nation expects to be ignorant and free ... it expects
what never was and never will be.

Thomas Jefferson

T homas Jefferson understood that a free nation depends on
an educated citizenry. Citizens must have the level of
knowledge necessary to make informed decisions on complex public policy issues. In the United States, schools have a major
responsibility for developing that knowledge.

In the twenty-first century, American citizens will struggle with
environmental questions of the first order. These include complicated and contentious topics such as global warming, pesticide use, and
species extinction. The goal of this series, Critical Thinking About
Environmental Issues, is to help young people recognize the complexity of these topics and help them view the issues analytically and
objectively.

All too often, environmental problems are treated as moral issues.
For example, using pesticides is often considered bad because
residues may be found on food and because the application of pesticides may harm birds. In contrast, relying on organic food (produced without insecticides or herbicides) is considered good. Yet this
simplistic approach fails to recognize the role of pesticides in producing food for the world and ignores the scientific studies that suggest that pesticides cause little harm to humans. Such superficial
treatment of multifaceted issues does not serve citizens well and provides a poor basis for education.

This series, Critical Thinking About Environmental Issues, expos-
es students to the complexities of each issue it addresses. While the
books touch on many aspects of each environmental problem, their
goal is primarily to point out the differences in scientific opinion
surrounding the topics. These books present the facts that underlie
different scientific interpretations. They also address differing values
that may affect the interpretation of the facts and economic questions that may affect policy choices.

The goal of the series is to open up inquiry on issues that are often
viewed too narrowly. Each book, written in language that is under-

standable to young readers, provides enough information about the
scientific theories and methods for the reader to weigh the merits of
the leading arguments. Ultimately, students, like adult citizens, will
make their own decisions.

With environmental issues, especially those where new science is
always emerging, the possibility exists that there is not enough information to settle the issue. If this is the case, the books may spur readers to pursue the topics further. If readers come away from this series
critically examining their own opinions as well as others' and eager
to seek more information, the goal of these books will have been
achieved.

by Jane S. Shaw
Series Editor

INTRODUCTION

An Earth so hot that it looks like an egg yolk frying in a skillet—that's the image the editors of *Time* magazine offered on the cover of the April 9, 2001, issue.

Inside, the talk was deadly serious. "Except for nuclear war or a collision with an asteroid, no force has more potential to damage our planet's web of life than global warming,"[1] it said. *Time* predicted higher temperatures, melting glaciers, rising seas, withered crops, and the spread of diseases due to the warmth.

The past fifteen years have seen the steady accumulation of evidence that the average temperature of the earth is going up. There is mounting concern that the cause is human activity and that these warmer temperatures could have severe effects.

Whether life on Earth is going to resemble a frying egg is another story, however. The theory underlying these predictions is that humans, by burning fossil fuels, are increasing the blanket of greenhouse gases around the earth. Scientists recognize that too large a quantity of these gases could raise our planet's temperatures, causing a cascade of changes.

Most scientists do not speak in the dramatic language typical of *Time* magazine or other mass media, however. The reports by the National Academy of Sciences and the Intergovernmental Panel on Climate Change (IPCC), on which *Time* relied for its cover story, are far more hedged with uncertainty. For example, the IPCC says, "In the light of new evidence and taking into account the remaining uncertainties, most of the observed warming over the last 50 years is likely to have been due to the increase in greenhouse gas concentrations."[2]

Some researchers are downright skeptical about the images conveyed by *Time* and other publications. Roy W. Spencer, a senior scientist with the National Aeronautics and Space Administration (NASA), says, "The popular perception of global warming as an environmental catastrophe cannot be supported with measurements or current climate change theory."[3]

The goal of this book is a challenging one—to look fairly at a problem that evokes passion and fear. The issue is not primarily whether there will be an increase in temperatures due to human activity—most scientists believe that at least a small increase is likely—but how big the impact will be. This book also discusses the often-neglected idea that there may be some good effects as well as bad ones and addresses what is being done about the problem.

Scientists disagree on many issues, not just global warming. These disagreements are as important a part of science as laboratories, microscopes, test tubes, and computers. Science is one of the few disciplines in which it is acceptable to be wrong because being wrong can actually be positive if it helps to advance scientific knowledge.

Critical Thinking About Environmental Issues: *Global Warming* asks the reader to step back from the headlines and look carefully at the

People join hands at an environmental rally on the island of Hawaii.

evidence that has been collected. It does not always provide solid answers, but fairly and accurately addresses the theories, facts, and implications of what is known about global warming. Because the issue is likely to be around for a long time, this book will provide readers a chance to think critically about the topic and intelligently follow the issue as it unfolds in the years ahead.

CHAPTER 1

What Causes Global Warming?

G lobal warming changed from a scientific topic to a public concern in 1988—and it has remained a public issue ever since. That summer was unusually hot. A major drought had shriveled farmers' crops. On a scorching June day in Washington, D.C., James E. Hansen, a scientist with the National Aeronautics and Space Administration (NASA), announced at a congressional hearing, "The greenhouse effect has been detected and it is changing our climate now." Hansen claimed that he had "99 percent confidence" that the greenhouse signal had arrived.[4]

Hansen's claim was picked up by the news media, and it resonated throughout the hot summer. The ensuing discussion launched a major government program to study global warming and marked the beginning of a new level of environmental concern.

The intensity of discussion remained high because, as the 1990s progressed, it got hotter. According to the most widely used measurement of temperature, eleven of the century's warmest years occurred after 1980. In fact, 1995 was the warmest year that had been recorded since regular records started around 1890. Then temperatures in 1998 broke the records set in 1995! People who sweated through blistering summers paid attention. So did farmers whose crops dried up.

The concern was tempered with confusion, though, because the 1990s also saw severely cold weather. In March 1993, a winter hurricane launched a blizzard into nearly half of the United States. It was

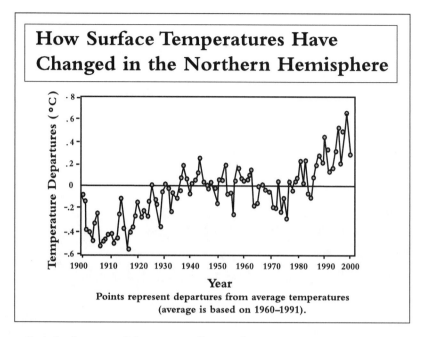

How Surface Temperatures Have Changed in the Northern Hemisphere

Year

Points represent departures from average temperatures
(average is based on 1960–1991).

called the "storm of the century"—until one just as severe took place in 1996. Some news reports linked the unusual weather to global warming, explaining that, paradoxically, an increase in global temperature could lead to more severe winter weather. With global warming, "extremes of wet and dry will intensify,"[5] wrote reporter Sharon Begley. Some went so far as to point out that if polar ice caps melted, the water they sent into the oceans could dilute the salt in the oceans. This could slow down the major ocean currents that warm the northern areas, causing serious chilling, especially in Europe.

As the decade wore on, some climatologists concluded that the greenhouse gases were responsible for changing weather. But others remain doubtful about the role that these gases play. The subject is much more complicated than simplistic statements suggest, and it is rife with scientific uncertainties.

There is no doubt that human activity is changing the composition of the atmosphere. Sylvan Wittwer, a botanist retired from Michigan State University, says it this way: "We are engaged in a great experiment. We are adding carbon dioxide to the atmosphere, and we don't know the outcome."[6] Yet Wittwer, more than eighty-five years old, has seen crises come and go, and he takes a calm view of this one. In fact, his research leads him to welcome additional carbon dioxide in the atmosphere because it helps plants grow.

Furthermore, a slightly warmer Earth might lead to more food, less severe cold, and better human health. Andrew Solow, a biologist at Woods Hole Oceanographic Institution in Massachusetts, once said that it is "ironic" to describe global warming as a problem because "it is not unreasonable to view human history as a struggle to stay warm."[7]

These calm reactions are at odds with what other scientists say. Yet even those who are alarmed about the chance of higher temperatures and rising sea levels speak in a more balanced and subdued manner than does the press. Stephen H. Schneider, a prominent climatologist at Stanford University, is convinced that governments should take action to deal with global warming, even though there may be some uncertainty; "I'm not a planetary gambler. I'd prefer to slow down the rate of buildup of greenhouse gases rather than gamble that things may work out all right in the end."[8]

Some Facts About Climate

To understand the scientific debate over global warming, it is necessary to know something about the earth's atmosphere, the mixture of gases surrounding the earth that we call air. The atmosphere provides oxygen for breathing and protects the earth against solar and cosmic rays. In addition, it keeps the surface of the earth at a temperature that allows life to exist.

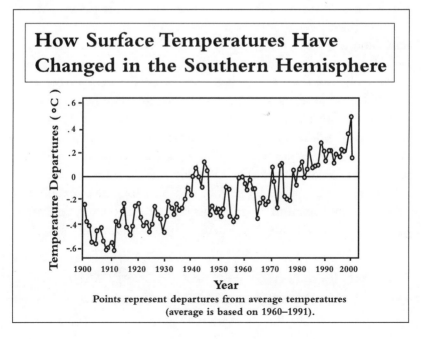

How Surface Temperatures Have Changed in the Southern Hemisphere

Points represent departures from average temperatures (average is based on 1960–1991).

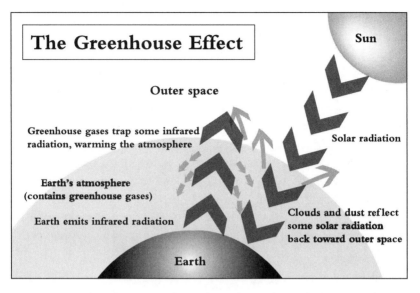

The Greenhouse Effect

Sun

Outer space

Greenhouse gases trap some infrared radiation, warming the atmosphere

Solar radiation

Earth's atmosphere (contains greenhouse gases)

Earth emits infrared radiation

Clouds and dust reflect some solar radiation back toward outer space

Earth

One way that the atmosphere does this is through the greenhouse effect. The earth receives energy—light and warmth—from the sun. As the earth and the objects on the earth become warm, they radiate their warmth back toward space in the form of infrared energy (energy that you can feel but not see).

However, not all the warmth disappears—and if it did the world would be cold indeed (33° C or 59° F lower, scientists say). Why? Because trace gases (that is, gases found in the air in tiny amounts) trap some of the outgoing heat. They are called greenhouse gases and include water vapor, carbon dioxide, methane, and others. Water vapor, which we don't normally think of as a gas, is actually the most important. More than any other substance in the air, its blanketing effect keeps our planet warm and livable.

The greenhouse effect is totally natural and beneficial. Its name comes from a greenhouse, a building with glass (or plastic) walls that is designed to grow plants. The two kinds of "greenhouse effect" are a little different, however. The roof and walls of a real greenhouse prevent heated air from leaving the building. In contrast, the earth's greenhouse blanket prevents heat, or energy, from leaving the atmosphere.

Out of Control?

During the past few centuries, human activity has been adding more greenhouse gases to the air. Although humans burned wood ever since fire was discovered in the distant past, the Industrial Revolution, which started in Europe around 1750, launched a major shift in how people lived. It changed the fuels available to them and harnessed those fuels to manufacture new goods.

For thousands of years, humans relied mostly on human and animal power to move from place to place, make their clothing, produce food, and form their daily implements. Then they began to use water and wind to power mills, especially to grind grain. But beginning in the eighteenth century, they began to dig for energy underground, retrieving coal that could turn spinning wheels, forge iron into steel, and propel steam engines. The goods and services—the automobiles, home heating, cell phones, and video games—that are typical of our lives today stem from that change in fuels. Some economists call the Industrial Revolution the Promethean revolution because it was based on fire—the gift that the ancient Greeks said Prometheus stole from the gods and gave to humans.

These fuels—coal, oil, petroleum, and natural gas—contain carbon. They are called fossil fuels because they are composed of the fossilized remains of vegetation and animals that decayed millions of

The Industrial Revolution spurred the rise of factories, where the power of fossil fuels was harnessed for production.

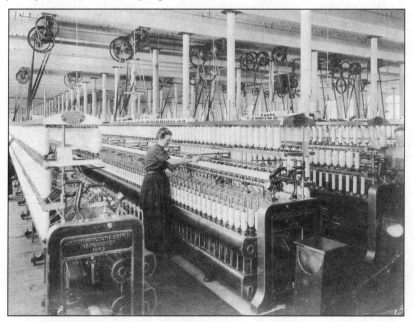

years ago and were compressed by heat and rock. In many ways, they are the mainstay of our economies today.

When these carbon-rich fuels are burned, the carbon combines with oxygen in the air to create carbon dioxide. The more fuel that is burned, the more carbon dioxide that enters the atmosphere. The levels of carbon dioxide in the atmosphere have increased from about 280 parts per million (ppm) before the Industrial Revolution to about 365 ppm, an increase of about 30 percent. As the world continues to industrialize and develop economically, fossil fuels will probably be the major energy sources for a long time. Thus, carbon dioxide is expected to rise to at least 500 ppm by the end of this century. Five hundred parts per million is still a tiny amount compared with the rest of the atmosphere. It is about one-twentieth of 1 percent of the atmosphere; today carbon dioxide represents even less than that. And whatever the worries about carbon dioxide, no one expects temperatures on Earth to rival those on Venus, where carbon dioxide permeates the atmosphere and temperatures are around 800° F!

As the world continues to industrialize, levels of carbon dioxide in the atmosphere are expected to increase.

Carbon dioxide used to be considered a neutral by-product of human life (after all, people breathe in oxygen and exhale carbon dioxide). Now that global warming has become a highly discussed public issue, it is often described as a pollutant. Carbon dioxide emissions from a factory are discussed in a way similar to that of sulfur dioxide or even lead or mercury emissions. However, this label is not really correct.

A pollutant is something that is toxic and harmful if one breathes or ingests it. Sulfur dioxide, lead, and mercury fit this description, but not carbon dioxide. Not only does carbon dioxide *not* harm people or animals on contact; it is what plants, including food crops, use to grow, to build their flowers, fruits, stems, and leaves. Through the process of photosynthesis, plants take in carbon dioxide, use the carbon, and produce oxygen. The problem with carbon dioxide is not that it harms anybody or anything directly, but rather that if there is too much in the atmosphere it will raise temperatures.

Greenhouse gases other than carbon dioxide have also been increasing as a result of human activity. The three most important of these gases are methane, chlorofluorocarbons, and nitrogen oxides, which are produced both naturally and by human activity. But "it should be noted from the outset," writes Arizona State University climatologist Robert C. Balling Jr. in a primer on the greenhouse effect, "that water vapor is by far the most significant of the greenhouse gases." In fact, he goes on, "water vapor accounts for nearly 70 per cent of the overall radiative effect."[9]

Water vapor is the humidity in the air, and its quantity varies tremendously, as anyone who travels from a desert to an ocean beach well knows. Humans do not have much of an impact on the total quantity of water vapor, but the amount of it in the air can change due to the effects of other gases. Indeed, what will happen to water vapor if temperatures rise is one of the key uncertainties surrounding global warming.

Over the past fifteen years, politicians have riveted their attention on ways to reduce carbon dioxide because it is more abundant than most trace gases and has a strong warming impact. The difficulties of controlling carbon dioxide, however, have opened the door to the possibility of trying to figure out how to control other greenhouse gases such as methane.

How Do We Know?

Because of the complexities of the global warming issue, many policy makers want to find a reliable source of information. Yet no single person or laboratory has all the relevant knowledge. In an effort to bring knowledge together in a way that is useful to policy makers, the United Nations and the World Meteorological Organization formed a group called the Intergovernmental Panel on Climate Change or IPCC in 1988.

The IPCC marks the first time that an international group of scientists has been formally organized under the United Nations to understand the science of a major environmental issue and to report its findings to government officials. The IPCC was formed because scientists were suggesting that human activity was increasing the natural greenhouse effect. Although not all of the twenty-five hundred or so scientists are climatologists (scientists who specifically study climate), they have been selected for their expertise on global warming, or—as it is increasingly known—climate change.

Are the governments of the world receiving accurate and balanced information? "Most experts view the IPCC's reports as a huge success story—the first serious attempt to reach a global consensus on a complex scientific issue," says Mark Schrope, a science writer. Yet, he adds, some people are uncomfortable. Scientists and government officials must interact when they write the summaries of the literature reviews. This means that they could be watering down the science or making the problem seem more or less dire than it actually is. They contend that this kind of scientist-government cooperation "undermines normal scientific peer-review procedures," he says.[10]

Normally, understanding of scientific problems develops through a process known as peer review. Researchers propose hypotheses—statements about the physical world that can be tested—and then they test them. Their experiments are described, and the descriptions submitted to professional scientific journals. Before publication, the articles are reviewed by other scientists who are experts in the same area, their peers. The best articles are published, and scientists respond to them, often by repeating the experiments to see if they come up with the same results (this is called replication). If they find flaws, they report on them, submitting their reports through the same process of review. This process is slow and is never considered final. New information and new insights are constantly modifying and refining the first discoveries.

So, even though the IPCC organization is highly respected, its goal is somewhat broader than the narrow research that most scientists engage in. The goal is to reach a consensus about a problem that is still poorly understood and to advise government officials on what to do about it.

After reviewing articles in scientific journals and preparing reports on climate change, IPCC scientists meet with representatives of many governments to summarize their findings. These summaries are what make "the news" about global warming, fueling the articles in leading magazines and pressuring presidents and ministers to consider action. The summaries, however, represent just one small piece of volumes that are hundreds of pages long. The IPCC has issued reports in 1990, 1992, 1996, and 2001. Some critics have doubted that the summaries of these reports accurately reflect the complexity of the reports.

Global warming experts summarize their findings at a 2001 IPCC press conference.

"It's a tough question," says Michael Oppenheimer of Environmental Defense, an environmental group active in studying and promoting solutions to global warming. "How do you provide a process that draws technical conclusions and is completely faithful to the science, but is still usable by governments? There is no simple answer." [11]

Temperature Predictions

What most policy makers—and the public—demand from the IPCC is forecasts, estimates of future world temperatures. The latest such prediction, issued in 2001, was that average global temperatures will increase between 1.4° and 5.8° C (or 2.5° F and 10.4° F) by 2100.

These figures may appear to be definite, but they really reflect a wide range of possibilities, ranging from hardly noticeable to severe. David Easterling, principal scientist for the National Climatic Data Center in Asheville, North Carolina, explains: "If temperatures increased 1.5° C, that wouldn't be cause for alarm. But a relatively rapid change in climate could have rather dire consequences over the next 75 to 100 years." [12]

There are many reasons for the range of forecasts. The main one is that scientists really do not know how additional carbon dioxide will affect the atmosphere. "What we do know," writes Richard Lindzen, a climatologist at the Massachusetts Institute of Technology, "is that a doubling of carbon dioxide by itself would produce only a modest temperature increase of 1° C [about .6° F]." That is not considered a major change, not likely to be felt as a significant change in temperature. But Lindzen adds: "Larger projected increases depend on 'amplification' of the carbon dioxide by more important, but poorly modeled, greenhouse gases, clouds and water vapor." [13]

It's that "amplification" that is so crucial. Increases in carbon dioxide are expected to increase the temperature of the air slightly, as Lindzen indicates. This warmer air will hold more water vapor, which is expected to keep more heat on the earth. But how much will the water vapor amplify the warming? Will it have a powerful effect, raising temperatures to cataclysmic levels? Or just a small one? There is even reason to argue, as Lindzen does, that it could reduce the warming rather than magnify it.

Another reason for uncertainty is that no one knows if carbon dioxide will build up the way it has been. The IPCC forecasts are based on the amount of carbon dioxide produced over the next one hundred years. But the assumptions about future emissions can change depending on how much world population grows, changes in technology (such as switching from carbon-based fuels), and on how much economic growth occurs. Perhaps people will deliberately reduce the use of carbon-based fuels because of worry about global warming. Or perhaps there will be a natural evolution toward fuels that don't emit carbon dioxide, such as solar or wind energy or even nuclear power. Or perhaps growing forests and changing agriculture will absorb more carbon dioxide than scientists currently think.

In fact, carbon buildup has slowed during the past ten years. Scientists then thought that the amount of carbon dioxide in the atmosphere would be up to 600 ppm by the year 2100, but now the IPCC expects it to reach only 500 ppm by that time.

In essence, each new piece of knowledge seems to open up other uncertainties. "Climate is not predictable," says Sylvan Wittwer flatly. "There are so many variables you can't control."[14] Yet predicting climate is exactly the enterprise that IPCC scientists are engaged in.

Svante Arrhenius theorized that carbon dioxide could raise temperatures on earth.

How It Started

The idea that carbon dioxide can raise the earth's temperature is not new. In 1896, a Swedish scientist named Svante Arrhenius first called attention to the possibility. He predicted that temperatures could go up by 10° or 11° F (which is at the extreme end of the IPCC's predictions today). For many years, his calculations were viewed as curiosities. Over time, however, as quantities of carbon dioxide in the atmosphere began to rise, people gave more thought to the possibility.

In the 1950s, scientists started measuring the carbon dioxide in the atmosphere. These measurements confirmed what most scientists thought—carbon dioxide levels in the air were indeed going up. Other greenhouse gases were increasing, too.

What really made global warming a major scientific and political issue, however, was the introduction of large, complex computer models that predict changes in climate. These general circulation models (or GCMs), are not models in the sense of physical replicas or images; they are complex software programs that take in information and produce predictions based on the information. They "speak mathematics." There are around twenty major models, located at many different laboratories such as the National Center for Atmospheric Research in Boulder, Colorado, and the Hadley Centre for Climate Prediction and Research in Bracknell, Great Britain.

These computer programs include a multitude of details about the earth's climate and the physical principles that drive them, expressed in terms of mathematical equations. For example, one equation might show that the amount of energy from the sun equals the amount of energy that returns to space, except for various intervening factors, which are incorporated into the equation. These would include forces like wind and ocean currents and the effects of trace gases and cloud cover. If the information about such forces and the physical principles that affect climate are accurate, scientists can use what is known about the past and come up with descriptions that mimic or "simulate" actual conditions on Earth.

Once the computer model can simulate the current operation of the world's climate, the modelers make changes in the information they feed into the software. Their goal is to predict what will happen if, say, a lot more carbon dioxide enters the atmosphere. So they enter a large increase in atmospheric carbon dioxide, usually raising it from the 365 ppm level today to 600 ppm because that was the level of atmospheric carbon dioxide they initially expected at the end of the twenty-first century.

Even though computers are known to have flaws in their ability to make predictions, no one wants to ignore them. Scientists began to report their findings in the 1980s, and these appeared to confirm what Arrhenius had predicted so many years before: Temperatures would go up if the world continued to burn fossil fuels and add carbon dioxide to the atmosphere.

Yet computer predictions still leave a lot to be desired. Thomas R. Karl and Kevin E. Trenberth, climatologists at two major climate lab-

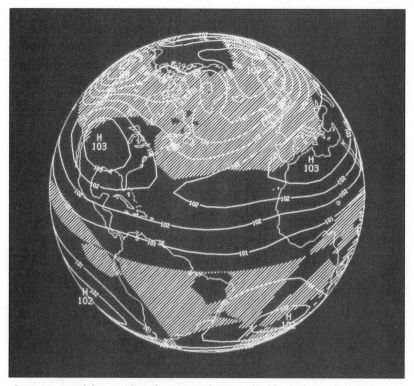

Computer models provide information that is valuable to climatologists.

oratories, say that to untangle the riddle of climate change requires "the technological muscle of supercomputers a million times faster than those in use today." This is the case, they say, even though the computers currently used "can perform between 10 and 50 billion operations per second, but with so many evolving variables, the simulation of a single century [of climate] can take months."[15] They are hoping that the importance of climate change will lead to a long-term climate monitoring program by the federal government, which they say does not exist now.

Meanwhile, knowledge about climate is increasing rapidly. Partly because of an infusion of billions of dollars of federal funds over the past decade, scientific study of global warming has surged. Almost weekly, important articles on the topic appear in scientific journals.

Conclusion

Predicting the future is difficult, and the future of the world's climate is no exception. So many factors affect climate that sorting it out requires vast amounts of study, perceptive analysis, and enormous computer support—and even then it may not be possible. Yet public anxiety about buildup of greenhouse gases, an anxiety supported by the scientific findings, has forced policy makers to take the problem seriously. Governments have called on scientists to come up with predictions about the future and to unravel the mystery of climate. This is a challenging task, and one that so far has not led to many certainties.

CHAPTER 2

How Much Warmer Is It?

Most climatologists agree that world temperatures have, on average, risen somewhat over the past century. The Intergovernmental Panel on Climate Change (IPCC) estimates that temperatures have increased by 0.6° C (or 1.1° F). Yet there are some troubling problems even with that figure. And there is a lot of uncertainty about whether that increase was caused by humans' production of greenhouse gases.

A temperature measurement sounds like a straightforward, reliable piece of scientific data, but global temperature records are averages of huge collections of numbers obtained from all over the globe. For instance, in the United States, areas of the Southwest show an increase as high as 1.5° to 2° F (or about 8° to 1.1° C) per decade since 1966. For the same period, other regions in the South and far northeastern states show more than 0.5° F cooling each decade. Only when such numbers are averaged with thousands of other worldwide readings can broad trends become evident.

And although temperatures have been regularly recorded since 1890, everyone knows that the readings are imperfect. Thomas Karl and Kevin Trenberth point out that sources of these readings include "buoys, ships, observatories, weather stations and airplanes that are being operated for other purposes, such as short-term weather forecasting. As a result, depictions of past climate variability are often equivocal or missing." [16]

Ground and ocean-based data are the temperature records that the IPCC relies on in estimating the 0.6° C change. The change was not a steady increase and, in fact, there was a period of steep cooling in the middle of the century. Nevertheless, about half of the increase (0.5° F) occurred in the past twenty-five years. The warmest eleven years of the twentieth century all occurred after 1980, with 1998 being the warmest year on record. It does seem to be getting warmer.

But there are some pesky problems that scientists can't quite explain. A relatively recent set of temperature records, collected by satellites, does not agree with the surface-based data.

In 1979, the National Aeronautics and Space Administration (NASA), the nation's space agency, began to use satellites to record temperatures between about one to six miles above the earth's surface. Initially, the goal was to fill in missing data to aid in short-term weather forecasting, but soon scientists used these data to calculate average global temperatures.

Both surface and satellite records agree that 1998 was the warmest recorded year, but otherwise they differ a lot. The satellite measurements show only about one-quarter as much warming as the surface records do. The increase in average temperatures recorded by satellites is so slight that if the record-breaking 1998 figures were omitted, the data would show a cooling trend.

To shed light on these differences, some researchers turn toward a third set of temperature records, drawn from weather balloon data. Weather balloons measure temperatures in the same region of the atmosphere as satellites do and have been doing it since 1958. Weather balloon data from 1958 to 1979 line up well with the surface data from the same time period. But weather balloon data after 1979 agree with the satellite data, showing little to no warming.

Naturally, the temperatures recorded by satellites and weather balloons are colder than those measured at the surface of the earth. But scientists are looking for a trend—whether the global temperatures are going up or down—not simply at the temperatures themselves. It is difficult to see why temperatures at the earth's surface should be rising while staying the same several miles up. Indeed, Sallie L. Baliunas of the Harvard-Smithsonian Center for Astrophysics points out that the computer models predict that temperatures at that level should have gone up "in concert with the earth's surface." [17] If the surface

Scientists use data from weather balloons to help determine changes in global temperature.

records are wrong, does that mean that the 0.6° C increase of the past century is wrong, too?

One possible reason for the difference is the "urban heat island effect." Temperatures are frequently higher in cities than in the surrounding countryside because concrete, metal, and asphalt retain heat, creating an "urban heat island." As the surface of the earth becomes increasingly populated and urbanized, some locations of the thermometers used to measure temperatures (such as airports) have become busier and more built up and may not reflect trends accurately.

Scientists try to compensate for this effect by moving sites to less developed areas and accounting for the changes. But Patrick J. Michaels of the University of Virginia and Robert C. Balling Jr. of Arizona State University argue that the urban heat island effect cannot be completely removed from the current record. They argue that there are other problems, too, such as "the lack of data in remote and oceanic areas, changes in the network over the past century, changes in instruments and observation practices, and microclimatic changes near the weather equipment, such as a growing tree near a weather station." [18]

But perhaps it is the satellite data that are inaccurate. Initially, these data showed a slight cooling trend from 1979 to 1995 of about 0.1° F. However, satellites change altitude over time (this is called "orbital decay") and several corrections were made in the late 1990s to account for these changes. Each one brought the data slightly closer to the surface data. Perhaps there are other aspects of the satellite record that need to be adjusted.

No one, including the prestigious National Academy of Sciences, a group of distinguished scholars that advises the government on scientific matters, has come up with a satisfactory explanation for the differences between surface and satellite readings. James W. Hurrell and Kevin E. Trenberth, climate analysts for the National Center for Atmospheric Research, think that satellites and ground-based thermometers mea-

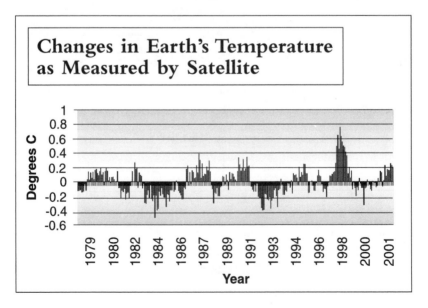

Changes in Earth's Temperature as Measured by Satellite

sure different things and should reveal climate signals differently. They say, "both give a different perspective on the same events." [19]

Human-Caused Warming?

In any case, most climatologists accept some increase in temperature over the past century as a fact. But is the increase caused by humans? The authors of the IPCC "Summary for Policymakers" think that a lot of it is. While acknowledging "remaining uncertainties," the IPCC writes that "most of the observed warming over the last 50 years is likely to have been due to the increase in greenhouse gas concentrations." [20] But not every IPCC member agrees with that assessment. "Distinguishing the small recent changes in global mean temperature from the natural variability, which is unknown, is not a trivial task," [21] explains MIT's Richard Lindzen, who doubts that human impact is yet discernible. He thinks that the computer models do not yet accurately simulate the natural forces behind climate.

Perhaps the increase is part of a natural fluctuation. The weather changes constantly. Regions go through long periods—even decades—of dry years and wet years. True, but to be in the warmest period of the past millennium is a distinction that should give us pause.

Furthermore, the warming may be accelerating. Half of the rise in the past five hundred years occurred in the past century. At first glance, it seems preposterous that natural fluctuation could explain a period that is warmer than it has been in one thousand years.

However, this warming might in fact be natural. One reason is that the global climate has been far from stable in the past. A related reason is that the world may still be "pulling out" of a cooler period.

Two periods in recorded climate history stand out. One is called the Medieval Warm Period, which extended from A.D. 700 or 800 to 1300. The other is the Little Ice Age, which extended from 1560 to about 1830. These periods almost certainly were "natural"; that is, human interference with natural climatic forces was probably not the cause.

During the early medieval period, for example (more than one thousand years ago), Greenland was settled by Vikings from Scandinavia. Later, it became almost entirely covered by ice and almost uninhabitable. Farmers grew grain in Iceland about the time

Viking ruins in Greenland provide evidence of settled communities in the past. Today, 84 percent of the land is covered by ice.

that the Vikings settled in Greenland, but they abandoned the effort in the sixteenth century when the growing season became too short. In Norway between A.D. 800 and 1000, people moved up the hillsides to log forests and cultivate crops, as much as 100 to 200 meters (around 300 to 650 feet) higher than before. Apparently, warmer temperatures allowed growth at elevations where it had previously been too cold.

Beginning in the sixteenth century, the climate began to get colder. Records show evidence of famine and crop loss due to shortened growing seasons in Europe. Permanent snow was reported in Ethiopia. In the Alps, glaciers advanced noticeably farther down mountains. These periods indicate that climate fluctuated long before human beings began to burn fossil fuels in the quantities they do today. Two scientists interpret those facts to argue that the temperatures of the past century went up simply "as the planet has recovered from the global chill of the Little Ice Age."[22]

When climatologists compare current climate to that of the past 10,000 years, they find that 7,500 of those years saw temperatures *warmer* than they are today, by as much as 1.5° F for 5,000 of those years. So, while today's period is the hottest in 1,000 years, it is cool when viewed from the perspective of the past 10,000 years.

Some scientists don't think this history is persuasive. For one thing, they contend that past climate changes were only regional deviations, occurring only in parts of the globe. For example, the Medieval Warm Period does not seem to have occurred in China or Japan. There is more evidence that the Little Ice Age was widespread, however, with evidence in Tibet, New Zealand, and South America as well as Europe.

Indeed, gathering enough records to make generalizations about past temperatures has taxed the imagination and skill of many experts. Thermometers weren't invented until the first half of the seventeenth century (by the Italian astronomer Galileo), so climate historians study remains from the past. They consult written records of temperature and rainfall such as sea logs and daily journals. Some of these written records go back to the ancient Greeks and Romans.

For earlier indications, they study the rings of fossilized trees, the levels of mud on river banks that receded because of droughts, rubble left by retreating glaciers, and so forth. The most reliable records come from Europe and Asia. Few past temperature records are found in much of Africa or from the oceans, which cover two-thirds of the globe.

Signs of Warmth

In addition to temperatures, there are other signs that support the view that the earth is warming: rising sea levels, melting ice, and possible effects on plants and animals.

The level of the oceans has risen during the past one hundred years. The primary difficulty in measuring sea level rise is that the land on which sea level is measured is shifting. Scientists must determine at what rate and in what direction the land is moving before they can figure out if sea level is actually changing, or just changing in relation to land. Fortunately, satellites measure sea level with much greater accuracy. Together, these indicate that the sea level has been rising at a rate of about three-quarters of an inch per decade or about four to ten inches during the past century. This is an increase larger than the past thousand-year average.

Another sign of warming is thinning sea ice. Beginning in the early 1970s, satellites began monitoring the amount of sea ice present in the oceans. Since then, they have reported a noticeable and steady decline of about 3 percent per decade. That is, sea ice appears to be melting. However, a scientist writing in *Geophysical Research Letters*, a specialized scientific journal, says that his studies of ice cover in the Arctic Ocean from 1991 to 1997 do not show a recent melting trend.

Melting sea ice may signify warming, but it does not cause the sea levels to rise. When floating ice melts, it does not expand the amount of water in the ocean. A simple experiment with ice in a glass of water shows that melting ice does not cause the level of water to go up.

Ice sheets are a different story. These cover large expanses of land, especially Greenland and Antarctica. If they melt, they can raise sea levels. When people talk of "the ice caps melting," they generally are referring to the ice sheets covering Greenland and Antarctica.

The retreat of the West Antarctic ice sheet (pictured) suggests that the earth is becoming warmer.

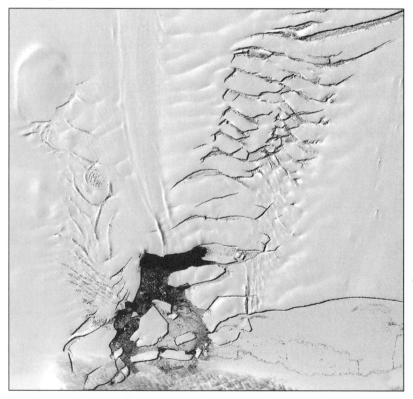

And these giant fields of ice do seem to be melting. The edge of the West Antarctic ice sheet is retreating, reported a group of scientists in 1999. However, the retreat has probably been going on since the end of the Ice Age. And in early 2002, scientists reported that the Antarctic has been cooling, not warming, over the past thirty-five years.

Glaciers, which are present on every continent except Australia, have been shrinking since the early nineteenth century. "Glaciers melting in the Andes highlands and elsewhere are already confirming the reality of a warming planet,"[23] say Karl and Trenberth.

Glaciers are masses of ice covering mountain valleys. They hold much less frozen water than do ice sheets. As they melt, they could increase water flow to the oceans, but the total amount of water is small compared with ice sheets. Strangely enough, however, decreases in glacier ice have been reported both in regions of warmer and cooler than average temperatures. Other natural forces such as erosion and friction contribute to the decreases.

Extreme Events?

Another sign that humans may be changing the climate is more difficult to pin down: Has weather become more severe, with more extreme events? Take 1998. Just about everything hit somewhere: an unusually severe ice storm in New England, fires in Brazil and Mexico, heat waves around the world, floods in China and Bangladesh, and the strongest hurricane in two hundred years. "While these examples are anecdotal," writes author Ross Gelbspan, "they are precisely the kinds of extreme weather events the current generation of computer models project as the early stages of global warming."[24]

Scientists have attempted to move from anecdotal examples to scientific links between global warming and hurricanes, severe storms, and droughts. Let's begin with hurricanes.

Dramatic hurricanes have plied the eastern coast of the United States in recent years: 1993 was the busiest hurricane season since 1871, with twenty-one named storms, more than any previous year. (Major tropical disturbances receive names from the U.S. Weather Bureau, such as Gilbert and Agnes.) The 1995 hurricane season was the second busiest since 1871; it had nineteen storms significant

A home destroyed by a hurricane. Some scientists speculate that recent increases in devastating hurricanes may be linked to global warming.

enough to be named. The year 1995 was also the Midwest's second most active tornado season, and it brought both floods and droughts.

Does this have anything to do with rising temperatures? It could. Warmer air temperatures increase the speed of the water (also known as the hydrological) cycle. This is the constant process of evaporation of water from oceans, rivers, and lakes. The resulting humidity in the air falls as rain or snow, and then evaporation begins again. If the cycle speeds up, water would evaporate more quickly from the earth's surface and fall as rain and snow more often or in greater quantities. So the result would be more precipitation. This doesn't necessarily mean more storms—it could just mean additional rain, which is often viewed favorably.

Precipitation in the United States has risen by 10 percent since 1910, according to a 1998 study. And over a similar period there was a 20 percent increase in the number of "extreme events" defined by climatologist Thomas Karl as two or more inches of precipitation in twenty-four hours.

Karl's report led to media discussion about a connection between warmer temperatures and torrential rains. Yet Karl's extreme events are not the same as severe storms or long periods of unusual weather. They represent sizable rains, but not much more, and they would be welcome in dry areas.

In spite of occasional peaks in hurricanes, Robert W. Davis of the University of Virginia says that there has been no trend in tropical cyclones and hurricanes over the Atlantic since 1935 or 1940, and no trend in the Pacific since 1960. The IPCC reported that "there is no evidence that extreme weather events, or climate variability, has increased, in a global sense, through the twentieth century, although data and analyses are poor and not comprehensive."[25]

Complicating the issue is the fact that property losses have skyrocketed in recent years as a result of so-called billion-dollar storms. Prosperity has led to construction of homes and other buildings on islands and coastal areas, which hurricanes hit. More media coverage, including a weather channel, also make more people aware of storm activity and its results. However, deaths from hurricanes and floods in the United States have fallen in the past few decades.

Animals and Plants

Another concern is the effect of warmer weather on plants and animals. Biologist Jerram Brown has been studying Mexican jays in southern Arizona for nearly thirty years. He finds that these birds have been laying eggs earlier each season—in 1998, ten days earlier than in 1971. Brown thinks that the reason is rising temperatures. Over the past twenty-seven years, the minimum temperatures in that part of Arizona have increased slightly (not the high temperatures, however). As Brown analyzes it, warmer temperatures in the winter mean that the birds don't have to use up as much energy staying warm. In addition, warmer temperatures may bring out insects earlier, which provides more food for females, enabling them to produce eggs earlier.

A Mexican jay. Changes in animal breeding habits may indicate regional warming.

Brown says that other species in the Northern Hemisphere are breeding earlier, too. "While no one study can prove that earlier breeding is caused by global warming, it all fits in,"[26] he says.

Other researchers have also found an impact from warmer temperatures on animal species. Norway's national bird, the dipper, has been increasing in numbers over the past twenty years. This may not necessarily be due to worldwide warming but may be caused by a shorter-term regional warming.

Warming in Europe during the past century could explain another phenomenon. Two-thirds of the butterfly species in Europe have moved northward, reports Camille Parmesan, a biologist at the University of Texas at Austin. "The only factor that correlated was climate."[27] Some butterfly species are turning up in Finland and Sweden, which were too cold for them to inhabit before.

Rising temperatures may help some populations but hurt others. For example, in Mexico warming temperatures are hurting the Quino checkerspot butterfly. Milder winters cause the butterfly larvae to hatch early. Due to the warmer weather, the plants on which the larvae depend for food become dry sooner and die. The larvae, now turned into caterpillars, do not eat enough to survive in their cocoons. One expert says that the butterfly would do better in a more northern climate, but commercial and residential development in California is limiting their habitat.

Warmer temperatures may be causing insects—including mosquitoes that carry the malaria parasite—to increase their range. In recent years, after decades of efforts to eradicate the disease, malaria has been making a comeback. It now kills more than 1 million people per year and infects 500 million. The main reason is probably the decision by many governments not to use the insecticide DDT because it may harm wildlife.

Could rising temperatures be contributing to this comeback? Yes, contends Daniel D. Chiras, an environmental textbook writer. "Warmer climates are already causing the spread of insects that carry malaria and dengue fever to higher altitudes and higher latitudes."[28] He says that malaria is expanding its range in Africa, and dengue fever, also carried by mosquitoes, is moving into higher land in Mexico and Costa Rica.

Could the fate of frogs and other amphibians be linked with global warming? From Australia to Panama, frogs have been dying out, and others have developed deformities. Because many of these events have occurred in places that are remote from human development, scientists have looked for global explanations, such as too much ultra-violet light or warmer temperatures. Recently, however, researcher Virginia Morell concluded that a poisonous fungus explains many declines of frogs in Australia. Her findings may not explain all the mysterious disappearances, but they suggest caution in assuming broad environmental connections to global warming—so far, at least.

Conclusion

So, it appears to be getting warmer. However, there is disagreement between records that measure surface temperature and those made by satellites and weather balloons, which measure the atmosphere a few miles up. Other events, from melting glaciers and rising sea levels, provide additional evidence that the earth's surface is warming. But they don't indicate that the warming seen so far is necessarily caused by humans or that the effects so far have been distinctly negative.

CHAPTER 3

How Serious a Threat?

A red sun pulsates over a field of withered crops. Torrential rains erode farmlands and warm weather melts ice caps. Rising sea levels flood coastal cities. Do such images accurately convey what global warming will bring?

One of the difficulties in answering that question is the fact that many outcomes are possible. The IPCC says that global temperatures one hundred years from now could rise by as little as 1.4° C (or 2.5° F) or as much as 5.8° C (or 10.4° F). If the results are somewhere at the low end or in the middle, they would, of course, be easier to deal with than if the highest predictions occur.

The high-end prediction does have frightening potential. There is a theoretical possibility that the giant West Antarctic ice sheet could collapse. This is a giant sheet of ice that covers part of the land around the South Pole. If this melted, it could cause a rapid outflow of water, raising sea levels dramatically over one hundred years.

A collapse might happen this way. First, warmer temperatures could cause a neighboring ice shelf, the Ross ice shelf, to become thin or even break up. An ice shelf is floating ice (comparable to a giant iceberg), so its disappearance would not cause sea levels to rise. When floating ice melts, it doesn't raise the level of water. However, the shelf may have a role in holding the West Antarctic ice sheet on the bedrock where it is now, keeping it from sliding into the surrounding sea. Without pressure from the ice shelf to keep it in place, and with increasing temperatures, the ice sheet could start to melt into the ocean. If this happened, sea level could rise by four to six meters (or thirteen to twenty feet). This would be an extremely serious matter because it could flood some coastal communities and low-lying islands.

Could it really happen? The scientists of the IPCC doubt it. Although the IPCC considered such a collapse as a possibility in its 1996 report, by 2001 the IPCC was more confident. It called a collapse "very unlikely" during the twenty-first century and suggested that it would take around one thousand years for such a thing to happen if it ever did.[29] In fact, the IPCC predicted that the Antarctic ice sheet as a whole is more likely to *grow* in size because more snow will fall.

The Ross ice shelf (pictured) could weaken and break apart as a result of increased global temperatures.

And then there is what journalist Ross Gelbspan calls a "rapid climate change event."[30] He points out that ten thousand years ago, a natural warming trend led to more snow, which then diluted the saltiness of the North Atlantic. This changed the density of the water, which then shifted the flow of the Gulf Stream so that it no longer warmed northern Europe. Within a decade European temperatures turned cold. Could this happen again as a result of human-induced warming?

The IPCC agrees that the circulation of ocean currents might have changed in the past, altering climate abruptly, possibly within a few decades, as Gelbspan suggested. Thus, "relatively sudden changes in the regional [North Atlantic, western Europe] climate could occur"[31] in response to changes in rain, snow, and runoff of water. But there is debate about whether warmer temperatures could actually plunge Europe into colder weather. In its 2001 report, the IPCC predicts that Europe will get warmer at least until 2100, even if the circulation of ocean currents weakens. The IPCC says that someday the ocean circulation pattern that warms Europe could halt, "possibly irreversibly," but only if the effect of global warming is "large enough and applied long enough."[32]

How Remote?

Part of the problem in assessing future impacts like these is that no one knows how likely the most extreme possibilities are. It's one thing to say that something could occur but quite another to say that it will, or even that it is likely.

Clearly, the frightening pictures of drastically changed weather patterns and flooded cities—especially from a collapse of the West Antarctic ice sheet—are extreme scenarios rather than firm predictions. The chances of their happening are quite small. That's not a reason to dismiss them, but to keep them in perspective. One scientist, Andrew Solow, attempts to do this. "While these possibilities are not utterly without scientific basis," he writes, "fixating on them seems to reflect a psychological attitude somewhat akin to a fear of flying," and he warns that allowing "apocalyptic scenarios" to determine policy choices may be a mistake.[33]

Even aside from the two apocalyptic scenarios, if scientists concentrate only on how warm it is likely to get, they face enormous uncertainty. The IPCC offers a range of average temperatures but does not select a best guess. The reasons are that the science underlying the predictions is uncertain, and no one is sure how much carbon dioxide will be added to the atmosphere. Climatologist Stephen H. Schneider is concerned about the wide range of estimates. He thinks that they convey a message that one prediction is just as plausible as another. Rather, he thinks that the IPCC should try to decide which predictions are most likely. He thinks that the IPCC should gather scientists together and come up with some kind of consensus on what is most likely. As he sees it, "substantial climate damage would occur"[34] if temperatures increased by as much as 3.5° C (or 6.3° F). He thinks that people should know how likely that is to happen.

Schneider published his request in a prominent journal. But two IPCC officials responded by saying that it is premature to come up with an "expert consensus." Sadly, no one knows the probabilities. Instead, the "full range of scientific uncertainty"[35] should be recognized, they said.

Whatever the doubts, rising temperatures could have severe effects. Reviewing the predictions of the computer models, a group of scientists headed by David Easterling rates the following changes as "very likely": more hot summer days, heavier one-day rainfalls, more heat waves, more drought, and more "heavy multiday precipitation events."[36] On the more favorable side, the models also indicate fewer cold waves and fewer frost days "very likely." Of course, these predictions are only as accurate as the computer models, and they assume that the world will be adding the expected amount of carbon dioxide to the air.

Often ignored in discussions of the future—and the images of parched earth and rising seas—is the evidence that global warming could do some good. Temperatures, for example, can go up in different ways.

Studies over the past forty years in the United States reveal that much of the measured increase came about at night rather than during the day and in winter rather than summer. Although the idea of higher temperatures elicits images of blistering summer heat, higher temperatures could mean something quite different. If warmer temperatures occur at night rather than the day, they could lengthen the growing season because night-time frosts in the spring and fall determine how long plants can grow.

Longer growing seasons would allow more crops to grow in additional regions—farther north in the Northern Hemisphere and farther south in the Southern Hemisphere. This could make a major

Icicles hang from an orange. Scientists say that agriculture may benefit from a shorter cold season.

contribution to combating hunger as world population rises. "If the warming is at night, that actually is largely going to be beneficial to the plants," comments Robert W. Davis of the University of Virginia. "The time from the last freeze of the winter to the first freeze in the fall is going to be a lot longer, because of the increase in the minimum temperatures."[37] However, because scientists still don't know *why* the warming has occurred mostly at night, it's impossible to say that warming will follow that pattern.

Droughts

What about droughts? Most computer models agree that globally there will be more precipitation (rain or snow) if temperatures rise. That is due to the quickening of the hydrological cycle at warmer temperatures. But droughts may increase in quantity and severity in some places. Higher temperatures could change air patterns, and it is primarily the currents of air around the world that determine which areas are dry and which are humid. Changes in air currents could cause some regions to become drier.

The current thinking is that the central part of the North American continent—where droughts already occur periodically—may become drier. Paul E. Waggoner, who brought together water experts to figure out how to respond to global warming, points out that the model they used "tells us little about what will happen at any specific location. Although it does predict that the interior of the large continents at midlatitutdes will be drier, it does not tell us what will happen in California or Iowa." [38]

There might be more droughts, or the droughts that occur might be more severe. "Much of the United States and Canada, for example, would be drier than normal," writes textbook author Daniel D. Chiras. [39] "If this happened, many midwestern agricultural states, now barely able to support rainfed agriculture, could suffer crippling declines in productivity." And Chiras contends that irrigation can't make up for this dryness in the interior of North America, partly because there would be less river water and groundwater. Although the northern part of North America would be warmer, the northern soils are not as good as in the U. S. breadbasket states such as Kansas, Iowa, and Illinois. "The optimum climate for wheat growing may move northward in Canada, but the rich soils of the plains will not be there to sustain wheat cultivation," [40] says journalist Andrew Revkin.

On the other hand, experiments show that higher carbon dioxide levels in the atmosphere increase the ability of plants (including many crops and trees) to use water. This could offset dry conditions. The IPCC emphasizes the difficulty of predicting where droughts might occur or become more severe. If temperatures rise as predicted, they "will lead to a more vigorous hydrological cycle; this translates into prospects for more severe droughts and/or floods in some places and less severe droughts and/or floods in other places," [41] says the IPCC. In other words, at any specific place almost anything could happen—more flood, more droughts, fewer floods, fewer droughts. And considering the enormous productivity of North American agriculture, even accentuated droughts would probably not be catastrophic.

Changes in normal air currents can cause severe drought, posing a serious threat to agriculture.

More broadly, with warmer temperatures natural vegetation could undergo changes. Observers point out that forests have always shifted over history as climate changes. Their seeds, carried by birds, other animals, and wind, can fall on good land and if the temperature is right, begin to grow. Scientists don't worry about the ability of forests to move gradually; it's the speed that concerns them. According to Andrew Revkin, a forest can migrate fifteen to twenty-five miles per century. But what if the forest needs to change its boundaries that much every ten years in response to warmer temperatures? "That is much faster than a forest can migrate," says Revkin. "In other words, a forest may be left behind. When that happens, a forest dies."[42] Something will replace it, but what?

Sea Level

The rise of sea level is one of the greatest concerns about global warming, topping even the chances of more drought and additional hurricanes. The IPCC estimates that the sea level will rise by the year 2100 by between twenty centimeters and eighty-six centimeters (eight inches and thirty-four inches, respectively). Although this is a relatively small amount, such a rise could affect the coasts of low-lying places such as Bangladesh, the Maldives, and Louisiana. Thomas Gale Moore, an economist who studied the potential harm from global warming, concluded that the people who live on coastal areas and low-elevation islands could be the only "major losers" from global warming.[43]

Being a major loser could mean a lot. Andrew Revkin tells the story of an official of the Republic of Maldives, an archipelago of more than one thousand small low-lying coastal islands in the Indian Ocean near Sri Lanka. The official was attending a UN conference on climate change, and Revkin asked him why he had come. "To find out how much longer my country will exist,"[44] was the reply. Most industrialized countries like the United States and Europe could cope with sea level rise and other warming-related dangers. Poor, low-lying countries might not, although the Netherlands has

Global warming could greatly imperil less industrialized, low-lying countries like the Maldives (below).

long used dikes to protect against the inflow of seawater. It built dikes long before it was a prosperous nation by today's standards.

Strangely enough, however, higher temperatures won't necessarily cause the ice sheets to melt. The higher precipitation that comes with warmer temperatures could cause more snow to fall in the polar regions, keeping ice sheets and glaciers from melting. David Malmquist, a climatologist with the Bermuda Biological Station for Research, notes that everyone is well aware of the potential for melting of the ice sheets as temperatures rise, but "what might not be so apparent is that accumulation rates also increase with increasing temperature, at least up to a point, and then they decline."

In Antarctica, he says, "a projected temperature increase will actually cause the ice sheet to grow." [45] This is what the IPCC expects to happen in Antarctica, too, although the IPCC predicts that the Greenland ice sheet will diminish. It will melt faster than it will grow with additional snowfall.

Hurricanes, tornadoes, and extreme storms have all been mentioned as possibly increasing in number or intensity. Clearly, some models predict that. Because warmer temperatures are likely to lead to more water vapor in the atmosphere, and thus to more rain, there is fear that more rain might come down in torrents, causing more flooding and therefore more erosion. But there is a great deal of difference between heavier rain and extreme storms. The IPCC stated that although more "extreme rainfall events" are a possibility, it is not known whether "there will be any changes in the occurrence or geographical distribution of severe storms, e.g., tropical cyclones." [46]

Deaths from Heat

Would more people die if it gets hotter? The IPCC says that higher temperatures could lead to "an increase in heat-related deaths and illness episodes." However, it also points out that there would be "reduced winter mortality in mid- and high latitudes." [47] The net impact may depend on whether more people die during extreme bouts of heat or cold.

Thomas Gale Moore, an economist who surveyed a wide range of weather and health studies, found that over a ten-year period, 132 people in the United States died from weather-related heat stress, whereas 385 died from weather-related cold. Moore concluded that warmer temperatures would reduce mortality, not increase it, in the United States, especially since the increase would be gradual and people could adapt to it. "It seems almost indisputable that Americans would be better off at the end of the next century if temperatures were 4.5° F higher than today,"[48] he said.

However, Moore didn't want to be misinterpreted. He emphasized that if average temperatures went up well beyond the 4.5°F figure, "at some point the health effects would undoubtedly turn negative."[49] Furthermore, most studies relating weather and mortality have been limited to developed countries such as the United States and Europe. The effects in less developed countries, especially tropical and semitropical ones, where people don't have air conditioning in summer and they work more hours outside in agriculture, may be different.

Two scientists, Laurence S. Kalkstein and Robert E. Davis, have also studied weather-related deaths in the United States. Their research revealed that in some cities in the United States, high temperatures are related to more deaths, whereas in other cities low temperatures are related to more deaths. Here's their explanation: People adapt to the temperatures in the cities where they live. When temperatures deviate dramatically from the norm, people die. So, in relatively cool cities like Chicago, which do not normally have extreme heat in the summer, very high temperatures can cause deaths. In warmer southern cities like Atlanta, extremely cold weather may lead to more deaths.

Benefits from Carbon

Usually left out of discussions about global warming are benefits from carbon dioxide, the gas itself. Yet the nature of carbon dioxide gives some reason to be optimistic about its increases.

In photosynthesis, plants take carbon dioxide in and use the carbon to create cellulose—the substance of their stems, flowers, fruits, and branches. As more carbon dioxide accumulates in the air, many plants are likely to grow more profusely. In fact, botanists point out that one of the limitations on plant growth—one of the reasons that crops don't grow bigger and produce more vegetation—is that the air does not have sufficient carbon dioxide. Commercial greenhouses often add carbon dioxide to the air to enhance plant growth. A long-term study at Arizona State University has shown that orange trees grown in atmosphere with added carbon dioxide are much larger than those raised in normal air.

Commercial greenhouses such as this one add carbon dioxide to the air inside, stimulating plant growth.

Botanist Sylvan Wittwer contends that if the carbon dioxide concentration in the atmosphere doubled, plant productivity could go up by nearly a third. Plants would grow "faster and bigger, with increases in leaf size and thickness, stem height, branching, and seed production. The number and size of fruits and flowers would also rise."[50] Not all plants respond to carbon dioxide by growing more fiber, but the most important food crops, including rice, wheat, barley, and potatoes, do.

The rising levels of carbon dioxide in the atmosphere are already boosting crop growth. Wittwer estimates that the carbon dioxide that humans have been adding to the atmosphere explains 5 to 10 percent of the increase in agricultural production during the past few decades. Simply sharing the atmosphere with carbon dioxide–enriched air has already improved crop yields around the world.

An added benefit—perhaps even more crucial—is that carbon dioxide allows many plants to thrive with less water. This is vitally important because lack of water is one of the biggest problems for farmers around the world, and warmer temperatures could bring more droughts. Plants take in carbon dioxide through openings (stomata) in their leaves. With carbon dioxide at higher levels, plants don't have to keep these stomata open as wide. Because these are partially closed, the plants lose less water and do not need as much rain.

Furthermore, if plants continue to grow larger, the increased vegetation will take in more carbon dioxide, preventing it from rising in the atmosphere as fast as it would otherwise. This phenomenon led a writer for *Technology Review* magazine to suggest that trees, shrubs, and other plants may be "a secret weapon against global warming."[51]

Not all scientists are reassured by these claims about carbon dioxide. Two important crops— rice and soybeans—do not respond very much to additional carbon dioxide. And some scientists think that the additional growth will be short-lived. Plants could benefit for a while, but then reach the limits of the "fertilization" effect of carbon dioxide.

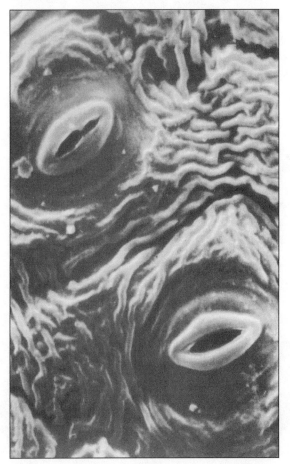

Partially opened stomata on this daisy leaf allow the plant to conserve water, making it less susceptible to drought.

Carbon dioxide increases plant growth unless some other nutrients are inadequate. One of these is nitrogen. In poorer countries, where nitrogen fertilizer is harder to get, the benefits of additional carbon dioxide may be weak. And at extremely high temperatures, some of the fertilization effect may be lost with all plants.

On balance, agriculture is likely to improve—as it apparently already has—from higher carbon dioxide levels. Less is known about natural ecosystems. Because plants respond differently to carbon dioxide, higher levels of carbon dioxide could change how plants compete with one another. Some plants may thrive at the expense of others, with unpredictable results.

For example, if forests are taller and more leafy, then plants that thrive in shade will do better than ones that require a lot of light, changing the composition of the forest. If higher concentrations of carbon dioxide lead flowers to bloom earlier, insects that pollinate the plants may not have hatched when the plants supply their pollen. Thus the plant species might actually decline, rather than prosper. Says a writer for *Science,* "Many ecologists believe it's too soon to say whether humans will celebrate or mourn the biodiversity shifts triggered by our changing atmosphere."[52]

Conclusion

So what climate should we expect for the end of the twenty-first century? There are many competing opinions, but it is possible to identify three main expectations about the future climate.

One group of scientists says the likelihood of harm is great enough that action must be taken. Michael Oppenheimer of Environmental Defense says that "global warming is novel in one respect. It brings with it the possibility of global disaster, and we have only one Earth to experiment on."[53]

Another group leans in the other direction, minimizing the likelihood of disaster and reluctant to take action without more evidence. There is "no substantive basis for predictions of sizable global warming due to observed increases in minor greenhouse gases such as carbon dioxide, methane, and chlorofluorocarbons,"[54] says Richard Lindzen of the Massachusetts Institute of Technology. These scientists do not completely rule out serious effects but expect that they will be small.

A third group predicts a continuation of current trends. The recent rise in temperature is likely to continue but remain modest. There is a "large and internally consistent body of evidence against the prevailing view of climate gloom and doom,"[55] say Patrick Michaels of the University of Virginia and Robert C. Balling Jr. of Arizona State University.

CHAPTER 4

A Careful Look at the Evidence

The key to the scientific method is re-examining one's hypothesis as evidence changes. For a decade, James Hansen, the researcher with NASA who kicked off the debate in the 1980s, has done just that.

Hansen's reputation has been on a roller coaster ever since he announced with "99 per cent confidence" that global warming had arrived. Initially, many of his peers criticized him for taking such a public role on a scientific issue. Yet, partly because he was so concerned about the issue and made it a political one, computers have been humming, scholars have circled the globe to examine bore holes and sea ice, and temperature records have been scrutinized and reviewed. Hundreds of scientific articles have been published since Hansen's announcement, as researchers try to figure out what is really happening to the climate.

In 2001, Hansen received the Heinz Award. This national award, named for the late senator John Heinz, is given to prominent individuals who have made a difference in a variety of fields. Hansen was honored, at least in part, for his "dogged pursuit of this pressing problem"—global warming. What is especially remarkable about Hansen is not his pursuit of the problem, though. Others are doing that, too. Rather, he is willing to rethink the global warming issue—again and again. Hansen does not shrink from revising his views if new facts are unearthed or new interpretations seem to fit the facts better.

And there are many problems with today's theories and expectations. Early on, Hansen struggled to figure out why the temperature hadn't gone up as much as it should have if the computer models were right. He also has investigated why there are differences between the ground-based temperature measurements and those made by satellite over the past twenty years.

He has considered—and reconsidered—how air pollution, especially sulfur dioxide, may be countering the warming effect. He wonders why the temperature record of the United States still shows no net warming over the past century, whereas the rest of the world does. And he has brought into his thinking new ideas, such as the claim that much of the warming could be caused by variations in the energy emitted by the sun.

"Hansen is a high-sensitivity believer and he did jump the gun back in 1988," says Robert L. Bradley Jr., who heads an institute for energy research. But he is also an "honest and distinguished"[56] scientist who has never been locked into a single position on this issue.

James Hansen continues to investigate the causes of global warming.

Today Hansen is much less sure that carbon dioxide is the chief warming culprit. Perhaps other gases such as methane have a more important role than previously thought. So, Hansen has been rethinking his early policy proposals to cut back on carbon dioxide emissions. That approach, he has said, may be too costly and politically challenging. Perhaps some easier policies—reducing methane, for example—should be considered.

Hansen's changing views of the global warming issue reflect its complexity and the need to reconsider assumptions at every step. There is more to be learned. The pieces of the jigsaw puzzle have not yet been fitted together.

What are the major global warming issues that haven't been resolved?

Not Warm Enough?

The biggest issue has to do with the difference between the warmth that has been measured so far and the predictions of computer models. Yes, most records show that it has been getting warmer, but the predictions of the computer models (the general circulation models, GCMs) indicate that with all the carbon that we've been putting into the air, there should have been an even larger increase.

"Simply stated, the warming has not occurred that is predicted by the GCMs,"[57] says Sylvan H. Wittwer. That is important. If the computer models can't accurately model what the temperature is today, can they accurately predict the future?

The world's atmosphere has experienced not only a 30 percent increase in carbon dioxide but also substantial increases in other greenhouse gases. Taking all the greenhouse gases into account, the world has seen the equivalent of an increase to 450 ppm of carbon dioxide, not just a rise to 365 ppm. With this much greenhouse gas in the atmosphere, temperatures should have increased by between 1.8° and 2.9° F over the past century, say Patrick Michaels and Robert Balling Jr.[58] Yet according to the surface measurements, they have increased only 0.6° C, or 1.1° F.

Why are there differences between what the GCMs describe and the actual weather patterns? One theory—proposed by James Hansen among others—is that the computer models are generally right but that they have failed to take into account sulfur dioxide, a by-product of industrial production.

Smoke containing sulfur dioxide billows from a coal-fired power plant.

Sulfur dioxide is a pollutant frequently produced when factories and power plants burn fuels, including coal. Sulfur in the coal combines with oxygen to make sulfur dioxide. It is emitted from smokestacks (unless it is captured by pollution control devices) and collects on very small dust particles in the air, creating sulfate aerosols. These dust-like airborne particles have a cooling effect because they reflect the sun's radiation back into outer space. Because burning fossil fuels produces both sulfur dioxide and carbon dioxide, these aerosols could be countering the warming that otherwise would be taking place.

This explanation, while promising, has difficulties. After proposing this theory, James Hansen subsequently concluded that the effect of the sulfates is too small to reduce warming. Later, however, he wasn't so sure.

The problem is even more complicated. When coal burns, it produces not only sulfur dioxide but soot—aerosols composed of carbon. As anyone who has worn a black shirt on a hot day will understand, these tiny black particles *absorb* radiated heat rather than reflect it as the sulfate aerosols do. Thus, the soot may cancel out the cooling effect of sulfate aerosols. Researchers remain unsettled on this question, and the ups and downs of the sulfate-greenhouse discussion illustrate that science often advances in fits and starts.

Another difficulty with the sulfate explanation is that sulfates should cool the northern half of the globe, which is more industrialized than the Southern Hemisphere, dominated by oceans. Yet satellite data show that the Northern Hemisphere has been warming more than the Southern Hemisphere over the past two decades.

The Timing Problem

Another challenge to the theory that carbon dioxide emissions are causing the warming stem from when the warming occurred. Although people have been burning fossil fuels in large quantities for

A scientist examines ice samples taken from the Greenland ice sheet.

about 250 years, the process accelerated after 1945, when the Second World War ended. About 75 percent of the carbon dioxide added to the atmosphere during the past 100 years came after 1945, say Michaels and Balling, when a worldwide economic boom spurred manufacturing and accelerated the use of energy.

Yet temperature measurements of the past century show that a lot of the warming had already occurred by 1945—in fact, temperatures peaked around 1938. And even though carbon dioxide continued to increase, temperatures fell for several decades, dropping over many years when carbon dioxide was rising.

This irregularity leads some climatologists to discount the earlier years as having any connection with carbon dioxide. However, as the warm temperatures continue, the argument that greenhouse gases aren't at fault has weakened significantly. Now, previously skeptical climatologists such as Patrick Michaels think that the more recent years warmed partly due to the effect of carbon dioxide.

Another puzzler: If higher levels of carbon dioxide cause temperatures to go up, then there should be historical signs of this. Scientists have bored holes deep into the ice in Greenland and Antarctica to study ice that has accumulated over thousands of years. At the time the ice formed, air was trapped in bubbles. With today's precision instruments, scientists can measure the tiny concentrations of carbon dioxide in those air holes as well as estimate the temperatures and identify approximately when the ice built up.

It has been observed that changes in temperature do not necessarily follow changes in carbon dioxide levels. Scientists from the Scripps Institution of Oceanography studied the ice cores in Antarctica. They found that over many thousands of years, temperatures sometimes changed first, before the amount of carbon dioxide in the air changed. When the last three ice ages ended, the temperatures in the air began to rise before carbon dioxide increased in the atmosphere. Thus, at least in these specific cases, the increases in carbon dioxide could not have caused the increases in temperature.

The Models Aren't Perfect

All scientists recognize that the models on which predictions of future temperatures are based have weaknesses as well as strengths and are only as accurate as the information entered. The forces affecting climate are complex and not well understood.

Hundreds of factors determine the earth's climate. For example, plant life in the ocean, ocean currents, and the atmosphere all influence how much carbon dioxide is absorbed into the ocean, yet no one really knows how much or how that might change over time.

Computer models make some predictions about what will happen in specific regions of the world. It is generally agreed that the interior of North America, on balance, is likely to become drier. But some regions within central North America could become wetter. The computers are too crude, even with all of today's computing power, to accurately describe regional effects. The IPCC noted that "confidence in the regional scenarios . . . remains low."[59] One researcher, David Legates of Louisiana State University points to a major model that has "lots of rainfall"[60] in the dry season in India and Bangladesh.

One sign of the weaknesses is that the predictions are constantly changing. From 1990 to 1995, the computer models' projected temperature increases—and related problems such as sea level rise—actually declined as the computer programs were improved. Then in 2001 the temperature predictions went up appreciably. The unanswered question is whether these forecasts are more credible than the others.

The GCMs might be wrong in a number of ways. Even though the modelers command massive computing power, the programs are still crude when compared with the complexity of what they are trying to describe and predict—the complete climate of the earth. So the information about the world and atmospheric forces may be faulty. For example, ocean eddies (swirls of water that can cover many square miles) can move heat around the globe, but they are too small to show up in most computer models, which describe broad regions hundreds of miles square.

Because the computers have to treat large areas of the earth as if they are of one elevation, their findings don't give good descriptions of regions that may be hundreds of miles wide. Mountain ranges have an enormous impact on climate; their cooler air causes snow and rain to fall, drying out the air as it moves over the mountains. Yet most computer models do not distinguish mountain ranges from prairies. The building blocks for the models are not fine-grained enough; the mountains have to be flattened in the models and the valleys filled in. The predictions for the wet, mountainous forests of the Pacific Northwest are not much different than the predictions for the dry desert in Nevada. Because they are unable to make such distinctions, the climate descriptions may be distorted.[61]

Even more important are the assumptions that go into the models. These may be flawed, because knowledge is always changing. One critical assumption made by all the models is that slight increases in temperature will have positive feedback effects, which means that one change will trigger additional changes that intensify the original effect.

One of these additional changes is an increase in water vapor. Yet MIT scientist Richard Lindzen proposes that if air in the tropics (where most of the global weather processes begin) became warmer, changes in the air motions would bring dry air down from much higher levels. This means that the atmosphere several miles above the earth's surface would be drier, not wetter. Without additional water vapor, there would be little warming. But this appears

Low, thick clouds such as these tend to have a cooling effect on the earth by reflecting sunlight back into space.

to be a minority view. Even so, David Rind, a scientist at NASA/ Goddard Institute for Space Studies, says that as long as measuring water vapor at high atmospheric levels is so difficult, "some uncertainty will remain in this most important of climate sensitivity feedbacks."[62]

Another question focuses on whether clouds will warm or cool the earth. Low, thick clouds tend to cool the earth by reflecting sunlight back into space; thin, high clouds tend to warm it. Right now, scientists do not really know which will predominate—warming or cooling.

Other Explanations?

While raising questions about computer predictions, skeptics are also trying to figure out what might be pushing up temperatures other than greenhouse gases. One of the simplest possibilities is that the changes may reflect the natural variation of the earth's climate. Reliable records go back only to 1890 or so, and that could have been a low point as the planet was warming from the Little Ice Age. That warming could still be going on. Or, taking an even longer view, maybe the gradual warming reflects a natural warming from the last "big" Ice Age, which ended about 11,500 years ago.

Another possible cause of the warming has emerged in recent years. This is the view that the changes in the earth's temperatures stem from natural changes in the amount of energy emitted by the sun.

First discovered by the astronomer Galileo in 1611, sunspots are dark areas on the surface of the sun. Although the sunspots are actually cooler than the rest of the surface, they are accompanied by a surge in solar energy. That is, more heat comes from the sun during high sunspot activity.

Since Galileo discovered sunspots, scientists have kept records of their numbers and found that they come and go in a fairly regular pattern—a cycle of about eleven years. People have attempted to correlate these cycles with conditions on Earth, sometimes to the point of absurdity such as using sunspots to explain business fluctuations.

Nevertheless, the idea that sunspots—or, more accurately, the solar energy linked with them—are major determinants of the variations in the earth's temperatures is plausible. "In other words, the mystery of global warming may have a simple solution," write author James

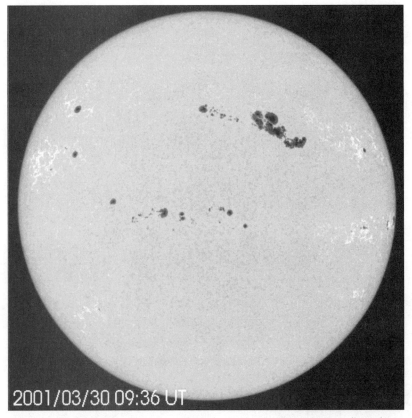

2001/03/30 09:36 UT

Scientists believe there may be a link between sunspots (pictured) and fluctuations in the earth's climate.

Glassman and Sallie Baliunas, a research scientist at the Harvard-Smithsonian Center for Astrophysics. They say it may be "the sun that's heating the earth, with its heat rising and falling in fairly regular cycles."[63]

The idea that changes in the energy from the sun could determine or strongly influence the course of the climate on the earth was initially dismissed when it was proposed in the early 1990s. But evidence that forced scientists to reconsider it turned up in an unexpected correlation.

It is known that sunspot cycles vary in length from less than ten to more than eleven years. Several scientists discovered that over the past one hundred years, the shorter cycles occur about the same time as periods of warmer temperatures, whereas longer cycles correlate with periods of cooler temperatures. The scientists who discovered

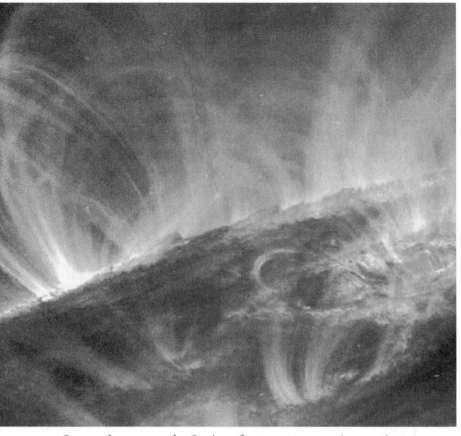

Surges of energy on the Sun's surface accompany an increase in sunspot activity.

this don't know why this occurs, but Richard A. Kerr, a reporter for *Science,* called this relationship "one dazzling correlation." [64]

Now a number of experts say that the varying output of energy, or degrees of "brightness," of the sun may significantly influence the earth's temperature. This solar variation is unlikely to explain all the change of the past one hundred years but it is "difficult to dismiss as a mechanism of climate change," [65] say James Hansen and others.

The fact that climate varies naturally and the role that the sun may play in that variation do not rule out human contributions, of course. These natural factors may be combining with changes that humans are bringing about. Some fear that when human-caused change is added to the natural warming, the effects could even be more severe.

As they put together the jigsaw pieces that comprise global warming evidence, it is easy for scientists—but even more so the public—to misinterpret short-term fluctuations for long-term climate change. This could be happening now. It certainly has happened in the past.

Cooling in the 1970s

Such a misinterpretation occurred in the 1970s. At that time, global temperatures, as measured by surface records, had been trending downward for thirty years. In 1975, a *Newsweek* article titled "The Cooling World" reported "ominous signs that the Earth's weather patterns have begun to change dramatically and that these changes may portend a drastic decline in food production—with serious political implications for just about every nation on Earth." [66]

Fear of too much cold was not mere journalistic sensationalism. The earth did appear to be getting cooler. Climate historian H.H. Lamb noted that "the temperature changes since 1950, small as they look in terms of averages, have affected the length of the growing season." [67] Springs in England were getting colder, and wheat farmers in Canada were experiencing earlier autumn frosts. This situation, widely observed, led to a book named *The Cooling* and to scholarly articles predicting a long-term reduction in temperatures.

Climatologists recognized that increasing levels of carbon dioxide were part of the climate puzzle, too. But just as important, it seemed, was the role of dust—air pollution from the use of fuel and other manufacturing processes. Writing in the journal *Science,* two scientists attempted to weigh the role of the two forces—increasing carbon dioxide and increasing dust in the atmosphere. They concluded that dust could cool temperatures by as much as 3.5° C. "If sustained over a period of several years, such a temperature decrease over the whole globe is believed to be sufficient to trigger an ice age," [68] they warned. One of those authors, Stephen H. Schneider, now predicts that the global temperatures will go up instead of down and has become an outspoken advocate of taking action to slow down the buildup of greenhouse gases.

El Niño

In the tropical Pacific Ocean, the atmosphere and the ocean interact to influence weather around much of the world. Trade winds blow from the east, pushing warm water toward the Philippines. This movement causes cold water to rise from deep in the ocean off the west coast of South America.

Periodically, these trade winds slacken or even reverse direction. This change is known as an El Niño, and it brings unusually warm air to many parts of the globe. (The name comes from the fact that the warmer air usually comes around Christmas, the birthday of the Christ Child, in Spanish, "El Niño.")

Sometimes El Niño can be large and powerful. Once it ends, and the trade winds go back to their normal movement, a colder period, known as La Niña, follows. This cycle of heat and cold correlates with cycles of drought in East Africa.

El Niño was unusually powerful in the 1990s, when it became famous. Because it brings warmer-than-typical temperatures to many

A motorist in North Dakota is rescued from a blizzard by a tow truck driver. Low temperatures in the 1970s caused global cooling predictions.

areas, it undoubtedly contributed to the dramatic warming around the globe that occurred in 1998. El Niño's notoriety has confused some people, leading them to think that it represents long-term global warming. The two are quite different.

Much needs to be learned about El Niño. Some climate change models suggest that warmer temperatures could lead to more intense El Niños, although the prediction is not a strong one. In any case, it is important to recognize that the two phenomena—El Niño and global warming—are two separate things.

Recent Confusion

Other examples can be found in which short-term events are misinterpreted. In 1999, drought in the mid-Atlantic region of the United States hit the headlines. This led some observers, including then-president Clinton, to treat it as a sign of increasing disruptions of weather brought about by global warming. Yet the extent and severity of the drought turned out to be overstated.

In 1999, less than 2 percent of the area of the lower forty-eight states was designated as having extreme drought conditions. In 1934—during the nation's dust bowl years—nearly 50 percent of the nation experienced the same level of drought. Indeed, at the height of the dust bowl in 1935, about 65 percent of the country experienced severe or extreme drought. That percentage has not been reached since.

In April 1997, Grand Forks, North Dakota, suffered a flood so destructive that government officials, including then–vice president Gore, raised the possibility that it might be an extreme event hastened by global warming. But the officials made a mistake, says Robert W. Davis of the University of Virginia. The Grand Forks flooding, it turned out, came about because there had been unusual snowfall that winter, and it was the melting snow that caused the flooding. As for the North American future, comments Davis, "When it's warmer there's less snow."[69]

The point is that it is easy to exaggerate the rarity of temperature and climate events and be misled into thinking that they mean more than they do. That is why scientists rely so heavily on careful measurement, statistical data, and studies of relationships. That is what science is all about.

Conclusion

The forces that affect the global climate are extremely complex and still not well understood. Changes in climate are subtle, confirmed only after decades of data are recorded, but the data are not always available, reliable, and interpreted in the same ways by different members of the scientific community. Careful study of these unsettled questions is an important part of the scientific process.

CHAPTER 5

What Should Be Done?

The subject of climate change is a scientific one, but it can be more than that. Environmental writer Bill McKibben, for example, is dismayed not just about the possibility of hotter temperatures, droughts, and sea level rise, but about their meaning for humankind. *"We have substantially altered the earth's atmosphere,"* he says in his book *The End of Nature* (the emphasis is his). "This is not like local pollution, not like smog over Los Angeles. This is the earth's entire atmosphere. . . . The air around us, even where it is clean, and smells like spring, and is filled with birds, is *different,* significantly changed."[70]

Other writers see global warming as simply a scientific question, one that needs conclusive evidence before action is taken. "The more I write about global warming, the more doubts I have about it," writes Matt Ridley, a science writer and columnist for the *Sunday Telegraph* in London. "Not because the facts change, but because the theory's defenders put up such weak arguments when you raise doubts."[71]

McKibben is deeply disturbed by global warming; Ridley is skeptical.

McKibben wants people to take action. "We must act, and in every way possible, and immediately," he writes. "We must substitute, conserve, plant trees, perhaps even swallow our concerns over safety and build some nuclear power plants."[72] He wants people to change. He agrees with biologist George Woodwell, who is convinced that the age of fossil fuels is over. Many who share McKibben's view argue that a lot of steps to slow down global warming, such as using less energy, will benefit people and their environment even if global warming turns out to be minimal.

In contrast, skeptics about global warming don't want to go very far now. "We would be better off spending our scarce resources in the pursuit of economic growth,"[73] say Robert Crandall and Fred L. Smith Jr., economic analysts writing in the *Wall Street Journal.*

To them global warming is not the mother of all environmental issues, but just another environmental concern that ought to be viewed objectively. They tend to question many of these issues, pointing out that other environmental fears—such as acid rain—have turned out to be exaggerated. This one may be, too. Often, such skeptics question government intervention and don't want regulations put into place without confirmation that the problem is severe enough to warrant them. Some are affiliated with industries that would be severely hurt by cutting back on fossil fuels; many are economists who tally up the cost and find it excessive. Others would like to address concerns, such as health in poor countries, that they view as more pressing.

"You have true believers and non-believers," summarizes scientist David Easterling. "The combination of the two makes global warming a big issue."[74]

So what—if anything—is to be done about global warming? Politically, pressure to take action has been building. An international treaty was negotiated in Rio de Janeiro, Brazil, in 1992 and eventually signed by the governments of the United States and 142 other countries, who agreed to work together to control global warming. However, few if any countries actually carried through with the proposed reductions of carbon dioxide emissions, which were voluntary.

Other international meetings, negotiations, and agreements followed. The most important to date is the Kyoto Protocol, named for a meeting in Kyoto, Japan, in 1997. A protocol is a detailed agreement that implements a more general agreement or treaty, in this case a treaty made in Geneva, Switzerland.

The Kyoto Protocol will not go into effect unless the industrialized countries that sign it account for at least 55 percent of the industrial world's carbon dioxide emissions (as measured in 1990). The United States produces about 36 percent of this total. In the case of the United States, the U. S. Senate must approve the treaty. Instead, in 1997 the Senate passed a resolution saying that developing nations,

President George W. Bush proposes a plan for reducing U.S. greenhouse gasses after the Senate rejected the 1997 Kyoto Protocol.

too, should have to meet the requirements, or else the United States would not support it.

Even so, the Kyoto Protocol is important. It could still be ratified, and it outlines steps that might be taken to reduce emissions of carbon dioxide and other greenhouse gases. These measures have framed international discussion and debate.

The protocol would require industrialized countries such as the United States, Europe, and Japan to cut back their total greenhouse gas emissions to 5.2 percent below 1990 levels (for the United States, the target is 7 percent, which means a very big cutback because emissions have continued to increase since 1990). Developing countries, however, are exempt.

The countries whose governments sign the treaty are supposed to achieve the targets by reducing carbon dioxide, methane, and nitrogen oxides. If the treaty goes into effect, the countries will have to pay a penalty if they do not meet the goals. The chief proposal for meeting these targets is to adopt government regulations that force industries to use less fossil fuel, either by conservation or by replacing current fuels with fuels that have less carbon. Congress would require electric utility plants and factories to reduce emissions of carbon dioxide in the same way that they require factories to meet tight limits on pollutants like sulfur dioxide and smoke. Companies would respond by using less fuel or switching to alternate fuels.

An alternative to requiring electric power companies and factories to use less carbon-based fuel is for Congress to impose a tax on each ton of carbon dioxide emitted. This would give companies an incentive to use less carbon-based fuel but allow them more flexibility than strict regulations. The tax would make these fuels very expensive, whereas fuels without carbon (such as wind energy) would not be taxed and thus would be cheaper than otherwise.

Whichever approach is taken, the prices of all fuels would go up, as manufacturers competed for the limited supply. Higher costs would undoubtedly lead to higher prices for electricity, gasoline, and products that use a lot of energy in their manufacture, such as aluminum. Even with regulations directed toward industry rather than individuals, the higher price of energy would spur people to use less fuel. "More energy escapes through the poorly insulated windows of American homes than flows through the Alaska oil pipeline," [75] comments writer Andrew Revkin. People would probably drive less, perhaps buy smaller cars, and cut back on air conditioning and heating.

The impact on day-to-day living could be high. After spending more on energy, people would have less to spend on other goods and services. For the United States, the Energy Information Administration (EIA) estimates that the annual gross domestic product (GDP), or the total value of what the country produces each year, would decrease by between 0.3 and 0.8 percent for a period of time, which could be a decade. Based on today's GDP, that means a reduction of between 30 and 80 billion dollars per year. Is this very much? The EIA says that although there would be "a definite slowing of economic growth during the transition period," the economic impacts would be "almost totally muted over the long term." [76]

But economist Bruce Yandle disagrees with this optimistic assessment. The growth rate of an economy would be cut by as much as a percentage point each year for a decade, he says, giving an estimate that is somewhat higher than the EIA's. Such a slowdown "is not small potatoes." After ten years, "the cost in terms of human well-being could be large."[77]

Supporters of carbon taxes or regulations counter that additional benefits would result. Air pollution would go down, and the United States would reduce its imports of oil. A recent paper published in *Science* claims that "adopting existing technologies"[78] to cut back greenhouse gases could cut deaths caused by air pollution in a number of major world cities by 10 percent.

A protester expresses her dissatisfaction with the U.S. government's stand on the Kyoto Protocol.

Trading Carbon Dioxide

Economists concerned about the high cost of the Kyoto Protocol requirements suggest a way to reduce it—by trading the right to emit carbon dioxide so that the lowest-cost method is used. To understand how trading works, keep in mind that the overall goal is to reduce the total amount of carbon dioxide in the earth's atmosphere. It doesn't really matter whether that reduction comes from many factories or a few—the total is what counts. Nor does it matter where that carbon dioxide comes from, because once it reaches the air, it mixes throughout the atmosphere.

Economists point out that different factories face different costs of reducing their emissions of carbon dioxide. For example, some factories are high-tech, modern facilities, so efficient that they require very little energy. Because they already conserve so much fuel, reducing it further might cost a lot of money.

At the same time, other factories are wasting fuel. For example, they may be old facilities with outmoded furnaces that lose lots of unburned coal in the form of smoke pouring through the smokestack. Simply replacing a furnace might cut back dramatically on emissions, even as it reduces fuel costs.

This is where trading comes in. An efficient company, say High Tech, Inc., could pay Old Smoky Co. to buy a new furnace. Old Smoky's new furnace would lower emissions of carbon dioxide at much less cost than High Tech would have to pay for its own reductions.

The actual arrangement might go something like this: A government agency would require each company to be responsible for reducing a certain percentage of its former carbon dioxide emissions. A company could cut back by that amount, or make a trade with someone else. If High Tech finds that it is expensive to cut back the full amount, it can look around for a firm that can cut back less expensively (Old Smoky). High Tech could buy Old Smoky's emission right—essentially, paying for Old Smoky's reduction. Similarly, a company that could cut back cheaply, such as Old Smoky, would look for a company that could pay it to cut back.

Yes, such trading is complex. But it has worked in other environmental areas, such as trading sulfur dioxide emissions, and many economists think it could work with carbon dioxide as well. Reducing costs this way would help to hold down rising fuel prices and soften the impact on consumers. It could even be used internationally. Countries that could cut back cheaply could be paid to do so by countries whose own cutbacks would be more expensive.

International agreements are tricky, however. Under pressure to get the best deal for their countries, and especially under pressure from influential members of each country known as special interests, governments tend to negotiate for their own advantage. "The treaty opens up opportunities for favor-seeking that were previously closed,"[79] writes Bruce Yandle.

In addition, enforcing these agreements might require an international authority to monitor the cutbacks and punish countries when they do not comply. Many governments are unlikely to accept this; they would consider such an authority a threat to national sovereignty. Moreover, Americans might not like the idea of transferring a great deal of money to other countries for this purpose.

Alternative Fuels

If adopted, the Kyoto Protocol would give a boost to alternative fuels—exotic sources of energy that represent only a small portion of total energy use. As Bill McKibben notes, nuclear power might even make a comeback.

Nuclear power produces heat by releasing energy trapped inside uranium atoms. Since nothing is burned, the production of nuclear

Power generated by nuclear reactors is one of several carbon-free energy alternatives.

energy is free of carbon emissions. This kind of power has been on the wane in the United States for many years, largely due to public fear of the hazards of radioactivity. However, nuclear power still produces about 20 percent of the electricity in the United States, and the majority of electricity in France. With growing concern about carbon-based fuels, suspicion of nuclear power could change, especially since new techniques for producing this energy are being developed.

Other energy sources could get a new lease on life, too. These include heat from the sun (solar energy), the motion of wind or water (windmills or hydropower), and natural heat from deep under the earth's crust (geothermal energy). These sources of energy differ from fossil fuel in that existing energy is redirected, rather than released by combustion with oxygen.

Although hopes for such power sources are high, they are costly today and they have their own environmental impacts. For example, wind energy depends on giant wind farms, which have hundreds of enormous steel pillars with fans or blades that can kill birds. So, although wind energy is considered a clean form of energy, not everyone wants it. Energy analyst Robert Bradley says it is "noisy, land-intensive, materials-intensive [concrete and steel, in particular], a visual blight, and a hazard to birds." [80] Others disagree, saying that most of the harm to birds can be eliminated if their migration paths can be changed. The Association of Wind Energy estimates that wind could provide 20 percent of the nation's electricity supply, although it currently only has capacity to produce about one-sixteenth of that now.

Solar energy, another alternative, can readily power low-level operations such as handheld calculators but poses real problems when it comes to large-scale energy. The sun's energy is so diffuse—so spread out—that collecting enough sunlight through solar panels takes up one hundred times the space required for an electric power plant, says Bradley. Based on current technology, millions of acres would have to be devoted to solar panels if solar power is to make a dent in fossil fuel use. Nevertheless, it too has its defenders, who are confident that if prices of energy go up, solar power will become competitive.

Carbon "Sinks"

As the costs of cutting back on carbon emissions have become visible, a completely different regulatory approach has begun to emerge: preserving forests.

Solar panels convert sunlight into a usable source of energy.

Trees and other plants absorb carbon dioxide as they grow. This absorption provides them with cellulose so they can grow, and it reduces the amount of carbon dioxide in the air. In scientific parlance, plants are carbon "sinks." Over the past decades, some of these sinks have been lost as forests, especially in the tropics, have been logged or burned, or the land has been converted to other uses.

Preserving more forests—as long as the trees continue to grow and take in carbon dioxide—might lower levels of atmospheric carbon dioxide, just as cutting back on fossil fuels would. This policy, called carbon sequestration (sequester means to hold in), could also help preserve forest habitat for wildlife.

Scientists believe that by preserving our forests we may be able to lower levels of atmospheric carbon dioxide.

Just as trees and other vegetation absorb carbon, the soil around them does, too. Some changes in agricultural practices could allow farm soil to retain more carbon. For example, some farmers use no-till farming—that is, not turning over the soil before planting—to keep moisture in the soil. This kind of farming also allows the soil to retain carbon that it has absorbed.

Carbon sequestration has a lot of appeal because it doesn't require drastic changes in lifestyle—just more planting and some different practices. Developing countries in the tropics like it because it offers a way for them to save their forests at a profit. In 1998, Costa Rican president Jose Maria Figueres announced that his government would sell environmental bonds to industrial firms. These bonds are promises to preserve the rain forest—at a price of about twenty dollars per ton of carbon protected.

Yet even this seemingly benign technique for limiting carbon dioxide buildup poses problems. For one thing, only when forests are growing do they take in much carbon dioxide: old-growth forests do not. Yet in much of the world, environmentalists want to preserve old trees more than fast-growing, young trees.

Britain's Royal Society, a scientific association, says that carbon sinks could achieve 25 percent of the desired reduction in carbon dioxide over the next half century. However, the society emphasizes that "this would require considerable political will." And the society worries that it would be a short-lived solution. The forests "will quickly become saturated, unable to soak up any more carbon dioxide."[81]

Then there is the political problem. The United States has many forests and extensive agricultural crops, both of which absorb carbon. Europe doesn't appear to have such large carbon sinks. European negotiators appear reluctant to give the United States credit for those sinks. Doing so would make it easier for the United States to meet Kyoto targets, while Europeans would have to rely more on actual emissions cutbacks. It is "not surprising that European countries would resist the inclusion of forest sinks for carbon monitoring under the Kyoto Protocol,"[82] writes forestry expert Roger Sedjo.

Is It Worth It?

Perhaps the most frustrating part of the Kyoto issue is the probability that if the industrialized nations go through all the pain of curtailing emissions of carbon dioxide, those reductions may not have much impact. NASA's James Hansen points out that the Kyoto reductions, if adopted, "will have little effect in the twenty-first century." In fact, he writes with others, "Thirty Kyotos may be needed to reduce warming to an acceptable level."[83] One reason is that rapidly growing countries like China and India are exempt from the controls even though they are expected to continue expanding their use of fossil fuels.

Even before the Kyoto exemptions were made, one scientist estimated that the proposed changes would have a tiny impact on climate change. By 2100, says Robert C. Balling Jr., temperatures would be less than $0.4°$ F lower than otherwise. This amount is extremely small.

Recognizing the hurdles to reducing carbon dioxide emissions, some people are seeking other ways to avoid catastrophe. Some years ago, there was talk of technological fixes to stop global warming, such as blasting sulfur dioxide into the stratosphere to cool the climate. Another idea was putting giant mirrors into space to reflect the sun's light away from the earth, thus keeping it cooler. But these sci-fi approaches have given way to efforts to cut back or sequester carbon.

NASA's James Hansen suggests that different irrigation practices in crop cultivation might be one way to lower methane emissions.

More recently, James Hansen, for one, has backed away from emphasizing carbon dioxide. He has proposed an alternative strategy —"to halt and even reverse the growth"[84] of non–carbon dioxide greenhouse gases, especially methane, and to cut down on black carbon soot. Hansen thinks that this may be more effective than cutting back on fossil fuels. For example, he suggests that the methane produced by rice cultivation can be reduced by using different kinds of rice, different fertilizers, and different irrigation practices. He thinks that natural gas pipelines in the Soviet Union, especially, are leaking methane and could be fixed.

Hansen's proposals represent an effort, shared by others, to find a no regrets strategy—actions that make sense even if global warming turns out to be a minor problem. Perhaps the no regrets policy most likely to emerge will be adaptation. This reflects the idea that people should respond to climate change—adapt to it—rather than try to keep it from happening.

To some extent, adaptation is inevitable. Economist William Nordhaus points out that people will make changes "more or less automatically"[85] as the environment changes. If coastal living becomes dangerous, for example, people will relocate or engineer ways to protect the coasts. If the types of plants or trees growing in a particular region change, farmers and foresters will apply different agricultural and forestry technology. Some farmland will become cheaper (because it is less productive); other land will become more expensive (because it is more productive). Changing prices serve as a signal, influencing people to do things differently.

Does adaptation mean simply waiting until something happens? Not necessarily. Researcher Indur Goklany urges action now to deal

If climate change alters our coastlines, we may need to relocate or adapt our lifestyles.

with problems that global warming might worsen. For example, hotter weather could increase the population and range of mosquitoes that carry malaria. Estimates are that the incidence of malaria—currently about 500 million cases per year—will go up by 50 to 80 million by the end of the century due to warming. But people are dying of malaria today. Goklany argues that combating malaria today by draining swamps and using pesticides could save people's lives now while making the impact of climate change largely irrelevant. If the rate of infection at 500 million were reduced by only two-tenths of 1 percent each year between now and 2100, he says, "that would more than compensate for any increase in malaria due to climate change."[86]

Similarly, other concerns about the impact of climate change could be addressed by attacking the problem directly. For example, improving agriculture in the developing world now means not only more food today but also more tomorrow, providing enough food to overwhelm any harmful impact from a changing climate.

Along with other experts, Goklany points out that a dynamic, high-tech economy will make adaptation easier. With better education, more wealth, greater entrepreneurial freedom, and generally better health, societies can be less vulnerable to any challenge, including global warming. "Virtually every indicator of human well-being improves with the level of economic development,"[87] says Goklany.

Conclusion

Global warming gives the appearance of being the mother of all environmental issues because it could affect the entire world, and the entire world contributes to it. The emotional aura surrounding global warming propels people to take action, even when the scientific facts behind the theory are still poorly understood.

Until recently most of the emphasis has been on reducing carbon emissions. Yet scientists concede that the proposals discussed and envisioned in the Kyoto Protocol would do little to reduce temperatures or forestall the other possible effects. And the costs could be high. This has opened up new efforts to cushion the costs, such as trading the rights to emit carbon dioxide, protecting forests, and addressing today's urgent problems that climate change might worsen. Meanwhile, research will continue, bringing the world step by step closer to an understanding of the effects of accumulating greenhouse gases. Whatever happens, the debates over global warming will continue. Their resolution is not in sight.

 Notes

Introduction

1. Michael D. Lemonick, "Life in the Greenhouse," *Time,* April 9, 2001, p. 22.

2. Intergovernmental Panel on Climate Change, *Climate Change 1995: The Science of Climate Change.* Cambridge, UK: Cambridge University Press, 1996, p. 39.

3. Roy W. Spencer, "How Do We Know the Temperature of the Earth?" *Earth Report 2000,* Ronald Bailey, ed. New York: McGraw-Hill, 2000, p. 39.

Chapter 1: What Causes Global Warming?

4. Quoted in Michael Weisskopf, "Scientist Says Greenhouse Effect Is Setting In." *Washington Post,* June 24, 1988, p. A04.

5. Sharon Begley, "He's Not Full of Hot Air," *Newsweek,* January 22, 1996, p. 25.

6. Telephone interview with Sylvan Wittwer, June 26, 2001.

7. Andrew Solow, "Is There a Global Warming Problem?" *Global Warming: Economic Policy Responses,* Rudiger Dornbusch and James M. Poterba, eds. Cambridge, MA: MIT Press, 1991, p. 26.

8. Stephen H. Schneider, "Global Warming Is Real," *Environmental Science,* Daniel D. Chiras, ed. Sudbury, MA: Jones and Bartlett, 2001, p. 486.

9. Robert C. Balling Jr., *The Heated Debate.* San Francisco: Pacific Research Institute for Public Policy, 1992, p.17.

10. Mark Schrope, "Consensus Science, or Consensus Politics?" *Nature,* July 12, 2001, p. 112.

11. Quoted in Richard A. Kerr, "The Right Climate for Assessment," *Science,* September 26, 1997, p. 1,916.

12. Telephone interview with David Easterling, July 17, 2001.

13. Richard S. Lindzen, "Scientists' Report Doesn't Support the Kyoto Treaty," *Wall Street Journal,* June 11, 2001, p. A22.

14. Wittwer interview.

15. Thomas R. Karl and Kevin E. Trenberth, "The Human Impact on Climate," *Scientific American,* December 1999, pp. 102–103.

Chapter 2: How Much Warmer Is It?

16. Karl and Trenberth, "The Human Impact on Climate," p. 104.

17. James K. Glassman and Sallie L. Baliunas, "Bush Is Right on Global Warming," *Weekly Standard,* June 25, 2001, p. 28.

18. Patrick J. Michaels and Robert C. Balling Jr., *The Satanic Gases: Clearing the Air About Global Warming.* Washington, DC: Cato Institute, 2000, p. 78.

19. James W. Hurrell and Kevin E. Trenberth, "Satellite Versus Surface Estimates of Air Temperatures Since 1979," *Journal of Climate,* February 1996, p. 2,222.

20. Intergovernmental Panel on Climate Change, "Summary for Policymakers: The Scientific Basis," January 2001. www.ipcc.ch.

21. Lindzen, "Scientists' Report Doesn't Support the Kyoto Treaty," p. A22.

22. Craig Idso and Keith Idso, "CO_2 and Temperature: The Great Geophysical Waltz," *CO_2 Science,* April 1, 1999. http://co2science.org.

23. Karl and Trenberth, "The Human Impact on Climate," p. 105.

24. Ross Gelbspan, "Global Warming Is a Serious Environmental Threat," in *The Environment: Opposing Viewpoints,* William Dudley, ed. San Diego: Greenhaven Press, 2001, p. 39.

25. N. Nicholls et al., "Observed Climate Variability and Change," in *Climate Change 1995: The Science of Climate Change,* p. 173.

26. Quoted in Bernice Wuethrich, "How Climate Change Alters Rhythms of the Wild," *Science,* February 4, 2000, p. 793.

27. Quoted in Wuethrich, "How Climate Change Alters Rythms of the Wild," p. 795.

28. Daniel D. Chiras, *Environmental Science.* Sudbury, MA: Jones and Bartlett, 2001, p. 491.

Chapter 3: How Serious a Threat?

29. Intergovernmental Panel on Climate Change, "Summary for Policymakers."

30. Gelbspan, "Global Warming Is a Serious Environmental Threat," p. 43.

31. Intergovernmental Panel on Climate Change, *Climate Change 1995*, p. 46.

32. Intergovernmental Panel on Climate Change, "Summary for Policymakers."

33. Andrew Solow, "Some Dyspepsia on Global Warming," Policy Matters 01-26. AEI-Brookings Joint Center for Regulatory Studies, October 2001. www.aei.brookings.org.

34. Stephen H. Schneider, "What Is 'Dangerous' Climate Change?" *Nature,* May 3, 2001, p. 18.

35. Arnulf Grübler and Nebojsa Nakicenovic, "Identifying Dangers in an Uncertain Climate," *Nature,* July 5, 2001, p. 15.

36. David R. Easterling et al., "Climate Extremes: Observations, Modeling, and Impacts," *Science,* September 22, 2000, p. 2,072.

37. Robert W. Davis and David Legates, "How Reliable Are Climate Models?" Transcript of Climate Policy Briefing for Developing Country Embassies, Competitive Enterprise Institute, Washington, DC, June 5, 1998.

38. Paul E. Waggoner, ed., *Climate Change and U.S. Water Resources.* New York: John Wiley & Sons, 1990, p. 2.

39. Chiras, *Environmental Science,* p. 489.

40. Andrew Revkin, *Global Warming: Understanding the Forecast.* New York: Abbeville Publishers, 1992, pp. 124–25.

41. Intergovernmental Panel on Climate Change, *Climate Change 1995*, p. 7.

42. Revkin, *Global Warming,* p. 136.

43. Thomas Gale Moore, *Climate of Fear: Why We Shouldn't Worry About Global Warming.* Washington, DC: Cato Institute, 1998, p. 128.

44. Quoted in Revkin, *Global Warming,* p. 128.

45. David Malmquist, "Sea Level Change." Speech given May 27, 1999, Washington, DC, Sponsored by the Cooler Heads Coalition and the Competitive Enterprise Institute.

46. Intergovernmental Panel on Climate Change, *Climate Change 1995,* p. 7.

47. Intergovernmental Panel on Climate Change, *Climate Change 1995,* p. 10.

48. Moore, *Climate of Fear,* p. 127.

49. Moore, *Climate of Fear,* p. 87.

50. Sylvan Wittwer, "Flower Power," *Policy Review,* Fall 1992, p. 5.

51. David Graham, "Plants: A Secret Weapon Against Global Warming?" *Technology Review,* July 1996, p. 16.

52. Elizabeth Culotta, "Will Plants Profit from High CO_2?" *Science,* May 5, 1995, p. 655.

53. Quoted in Revkin, *Global Warming,* p. 115.

54. Richard Lindzen, "Global Warming: The Origin and Nature of the Alleged Scientific Consensus," *Regulation,* Spring 1992, p. 87.

55. Michaels and Balling, *The Satanic Gases,* p. 4.

Chapter 4: A Careful Look at the Evidence

56. E-mail from Robert L. Bradley Jr. to the author, February 8, 2001.

57. Sylvan H. Wittwer, *Food, Climate, and Carbon Dioxide: The Global Environment and World Food Production.* Boca Raton, FL: Lewis Publishers, 1995, p. 50.

58. Michaels and Balling, *The Satanic Gases,* p. 36.

59. A. Kattenberg, F. Giorgi, and H. Grassl, "Climate Models—Projections of Future Climate," in *Climate Change 1995: The Science of Climate Change,* p. 339.

60. Davis and Legates, "How Reliable Are Climate Models?"

61. Robert Jastrow, William Nierenberg, and Frederick Seitz, *Scientific Perspectives on the Greenhouse Problem.* Ottawa, IL: Jameson Books, 1990, pp. 11–12.

62. David Rind, "Just Add Water Vapor," *Science,* August 21, 1998, p. 1,153.

63. Glassman and Baliunas, "Bush Is Right on Global Warming," p. 29.

64. Richard A. Kerr, "Could the Sun Be Warming the Climate?" *Science,* November 1, 1991, p. 652.

65. James Hansen, Reto Ruedy, Jay Glascoe, and Makiko Sato, "Whither U.S. Climate?" NASA Goddard Institute for Space Studies, February 1, 2001. www.giss.nasa.gov.

66. Peter Gwynne, "The Cooling World," *Newsweek,* April 28, 1975, p. 64.

67. H.H. Lamb, *Climate, History, and the Modern World.* New York: Methuen, 1982, p. 262.

68. S.I. Rasool and S.H. Schneider, "Atmospheric Carbon Dioxide and Aerosols: Effects of Large Increases on Global Climate," *Science,* July 9, 1972, p. 138.

69. Davis and Legates, "How Reliable Are Climate Models?"

Chapter 5: What Should Be Done?

70. Bill McKibben, *The End of Nature.* New York: Doubleday, 1989, p. 18.

71. Matt Ridley, *Down to Earth: A Contrarian View of Environmental Problems.* London: Institute for Economic Affairs, 1995, p. 25.

72. McKibben, *The End of Nature,* p. 146.

73. Robert Crandall and Fred L. Smith Jr., "CO_2 Controls Are a Bad Idea, 'Voluntary' or Not," *Wall Street Journal,* July 31, 2001.

74. Telephone interview with David Easterling.

75. Revkin, *Global Warming,* p. 146.

76. Energy Information Administration, Department of Energy, "What Does the Kyoto Protocol Mean to U.S. Energy Markets and the U.S. Economy?" Report prepared for the Committee on Science, U.S. House of Representatives, 1998, p. 65.

77. Bruce Yandle, "Bootleggers, Baptists, and Global Warming," *PERC Policy Series* PS-14, Bozeman, MT: PERC, November 1998, p. 14.

78. Luis Cifuentes et al., "Hidden Health Benefits of Greenhouse Gas Mitigation," *Science,* August 17, 2001, p. 1,257.

79. Yandle, "Bootleggers, Baptists, and Global Warming," p. 2.

80. Robert L. Bradley Jr., "Renewable Energy: Not Cheap, Not 'Green,'" *Cato Policy Analysis No. 280,* Washington, DC: Cato Institute, August 27, 1997, p. 6.

81. "Royal Society Disputes Value of Carbon Sinks," *Nature,* July 12, 2001, p. 108.

82. Roger Sedjo, "Forest 'Sinks' as a Tool for Climate Change Policy," *Resources,* Spring 2001.

83. James E. Hansen, Makiko Sato, Reto Ruedy et al., "Global Warming in the 21st Century: An Alternative Scenario." NASA Goddard Institute for Space Studies, April 17, 2001. www.giss. nasa.gov.

84. Hansen et al., "Global Warming in the 21st Century: An Alternative Scenario."

85. W. D. Nordhaus, "Economic Approaches to Greenhouse Warming," *Global Warming: Economic Policy Approaches,* Rudiger D. Dornbush and James M. Poterba, eds. Cambridge, MA: MIT Press, 1991, p. 52.

86. Indur M. Goklany, "Applying the Precautionary Principle to Global Warming." *Policy Study No. 158.* St. Louis, MO: Center for the Study of American Business, November 2000, p. 20.

87. Goklany, "Applying the Precautionary Principle to Global Warming," p. 15.

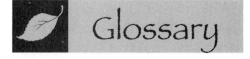 Glossary

Adaptation: coping with a problem, such as global warming, by a gradual response as specific difficulties occur.

Alternative fuels: sources of energy that are relatively rare today, such as solar and wind energy.

Carbon dioxide: a trace gas in the atmosphere that is believed to contribute to global warming; it is formed when carbon-rich fuels combine with oxygen in the air through combustion.

Carbon sequestration: the process by which trees, other vegetation, and soil hold carbon in the form of plant matter, preventing the formation of carbon dioxide.

Carbon sinks: plants or other material, such as soil, that absorb and retain carbon.

Carbon tax: a tax placed on fuel, based on the amount of carbon in the fuel; it is designed to discourage the use of fuel that produces carbon dioxide.

CFCs: chlorofluorocarbons, synthetic chemicals that remain in the atmosphere and may contribute to global warming.

El Niño: a change in the direction of the tropical trade winds, bringing unusually warm air to much of the world.

Emissions trading: exchanging the right to produce a certain amount of a by-product (such as carbon dioxide); companies that find reducing the emissions to be costly can pay others to reduce their emissions, so both parties benefit.

GCMs: general circulation models, giant computer software programs that describe the forces of the climate.

Glacier: a mass of ice formed by snow that falls and accumulates.

Global warming: rising average world temperatures, often attributed to increases in greenhouse gases.

Greenhouse effect: the warming of the earth by water and trace gases, which keep some energy on the earth's surface, rather than allow it to go into outer space. This is a natural phenomenon to which human activities may contribute.

Greenhouse gases: gases in the atmosphere that warm the earth by keeping some energy emitted by objects on the earth from escaping; they include water vapor, carbon dioxide, methane, nitrogen oxides, CFCs, and a few others.

Hydrological cycle: the movement of water from the surface of the earth through the atmosphere and back to the earth; also called the water cycle.

Ice Age: one of the periods, lasting between 60,000 and 100,000 years, in which the earth is much colder than it is today; we are currently in an interglacial or warmer period between the Ice Ages; it began about 11,500 years ago.

Ice sheets: thick sheets of ice covering a large part of a land mass such as Greenland or Antarctica.

IPCC: Intergovernmental Panel on Climate Change, an organization of scientists formed by the United Nations Environment Programme and the World Metereological Organization.

Kyoto Protocol: an international agreement negotiated in 1997 that, if signed by sufficient industrial nations, will require cutbacks in the amount of carbon dioxide emitted by each participating country.

La Niña: a return of the tropical trade winds to their usual direction, following an El Niño.

Little Ice Age: a period of temperatures somewhat cooler than today, usually dated from about A.D. 1560 to 1830.

Medieval Warm Period: a period of temperatures somewhat warmer than today, usually dated from A.D. 700 or 800 to 1300.

Methane: the major constituent of the fuel "natural gas," as well as a gas produced by chemical processes in wetlands and rice cultivation.

Nitrogen oxides: trace gases produced by combustion that also have a greenhouse effect.

No regrets policy: ways of dealing with potential global warming that will not cause harm if global warming turns out not to be a serious problem.

Photosynthesis: a chemical process by which plants convert sunlight, water, and nutrients into organic matter, taking carbon dioxide from the atmosphere and emitting oxygen to the atmosphere.

Urban heat island effect: the increase in air temperature due to the warmth generated by a city's activity and energy use.

For Further Reading

Books

Intergovernmental Panel on Climate Change, *Climate Change 1995: The Science of Climate Change,* 1996. Cambridge, UK: Cambridge University Press. A comprehensive report from the international organization that reviews the science of global warming.

Intergovernmental Panel on Climate Change, *Climate Change 2001: The Scientific Basis.* 2001. Cambridge, UK: Cambridge University Press, 2001. The latest report of the international organization that reviews the science of global warming.

H.H. Lamb, *Climate, History, and the Modern World.* New York: Methuen, 1982. A discussion by an acknowledged expert explaining what is known about climate history.

Patrick J. Michaels and Robert C. Balling Jr., *The Satanic Gases: Clearing the Air About Global Warming.* Washington, DC: Cato Institute, 2000. Discussion of global warming by two climatologists who doubt that global warming is going to be catastrophic.

Thomas Gale Moore, *Climate of Fear: Why We Shouldn't Worry About Global Warming.* Washington, DC: Cato Institute, 1998. An economist argues that a warmer world won't be so bad.

Andrew Revkin, *Global Warming: Understanding the Forecast.* New York: Abbeville Publishers, 1992. A readable overview of the more severe possible outcomes.

Stephen H. Schneider, ed., *Climate Change Policy: A Survey.* Washington, DC: Island Press. A new collection of essays selected by a leading proponent of policies to combat global warming.

Periodicals

Richard Lindzen, "Global Warming: The Origin and Nature of the Alleged Scientific Consensus," *Regulation,* Spring 1992.

Stephen H. Schneider, Arthur Rosencranz, and John O. Niles, eds. "The Greenhouse Effect: Science and Policy," *Science,* February 10, 1989.

Internet Sources

AEI–Brookings Joint Center for Regulatory Studies (www.aei. brooking.org).

CO_2 Science (http://co2science.org).

Environmental Protection Agency (www.epa.gov).

Greening Earth Society (www.greeningearthsociety.org).

U.S. Global Climate Research Program (www.USGCRP.gov).

Works Consulted

Books

Robert C. Balling Jr., "Global Warming: Messy Models, Decent Data, and Pointless Policy," *The True State of the Planet,* Ronald Bailey, ed. New York: The Free Press, 1995.

——, *The Heated Debate.* San Francisco: Pacific Research Institute for Public Policy, 1992.

——, "Measures to Combat Global Warming Should Be Delayed," *Global Warming: Opposing Viewpoints,* Tamara L. Roleff, ed. San Diego: Greenhaven Press, 1997.

Robert J. Bradley Jr., *Julian Simon and the Triumph of Energy Sustainability.* Washington, DC: American Legislative Exchange Council, 2000.

Daniel D. Chiras, *Environmental Science.* Sudbury, MA: Jones and Bartlett, 2001.

Ross Gelbspan, "Global Warming Is a Serious Environmental Threat," *The Environment: Opposing Viewpoints,* William Dudley, ed. San Diego: Greenhaven Press, 2001.

Robert Jastrow, William Nierenberg, and Frederick Seitz, *Scientific Perspectives on the Greenhouse Problem.* Ottawa, IL: Jameson Books, 1990.

John McCarthy, *Frequently Asked Questions About Nuclear Energy.* Stanford, CA: Stanford University, 1995.

Bill McKibben, *The End of Nature.* New York: Doubleday, 1989.

George J. Mitchell, "The Effects of Global Warming Will Be Detrimental," *Global Warming: Opposing Viewpoints,* Tamara L. Roleff, ed. San Diego: Greenhaven Press, 1997.

National Research Council, *Reconciling Observations of Global Temperature Change.* Washington, DC: National Academy Press, 2000.

Annika Nilsson, *Greenhouse Earth.* New York: John Wiley and Sons, 1992.

W.D. Nordhaus, "Economic Approaches to Greenhouse Warming," *Global Warming: Economic Policy Approaches*, Rudiger D. Dornbush and James M. Poterba, eds. Cambridge, MA: MIT Press, 1991.

Matt Ridley, *Down to Earth: A Contrarian View of Environmental Problems*. London: Institute for Economic Affairs, 1995.

Stephen H. Schneider, *The Genesis Strategy: Climate and Global Survival*. New York: Plenum Press, 1976.

———, "Global Warming Is Real," *Environmental Science*, Daniel D. Chiras, ed. Sudbury, MA: Jones and Bartlett, 2001.

S. Fred Singer, *Climate Policy from Rio to Kyoto—A Political Issue for 2000 and Beyond*. Stanford, CA: Hoover Institution Press, 2000.

Andrew Solow, "Is There a Global Warming Problem?" *Global Warming: Economic Policy Responses*, Rudiger Dornbusch and James M. Poterba, eds. Cambridge, MA: MIT Press, 1991.

Roy W. Spencer, "How Do We Know the Temperature of the Earth? Global Warming and Global Temperatures," *Earth Report 2000*, Ronald Bailey, ed. New York: McGraw-Hill, 2000.

David D. Victor, *The Collapse of the Kyoto Protocol and the Struggle to Slow Global Warming*. Princeton, NJ: Princeton University Press, 2001.

Paul E. Waggoner, *Climate Change and U.S. Water Resources*. New York: John Wiley & Sons, 1990.

Robert T. Watson, "Global Warming Poses a Serious Threat," *Global Warming: Opposing Viewpoints*, Tamara L. Roleff, ed. San Diego: Greenhaven Press, 1997.

Sylvan H. Wittwer, *Food, Climate, and Carbon Dioxide: The Global Environment and World Food Production*. Boca Raton, FL: Lewis Publishers, 1995.

Periodicals

Meinrat O. Andreae, "The Dark Side of Aerosols," *Nature*, February 8, 2001.

Sharon Begley, "He's Not Full of Hot Air," *Newsweek*, January 22, 1996.

Robert L. Bradley Jr., "Renewable Energy: Not Cheap, Not 'Green,'" *Cato Policy Analysis No. 280.* Washington, DC: Cato Institute, August 27, 1997.

Luis Cifuentes, Victor H. Borja-Aburto, Nelson Gouvela et al., "Hidden Health Benefits of Greenhouse Gas Mitigation," *Science,* August 17, 2001.

H. Conway, B.L. Hall, G.H. Denton et al., "Past and Future Grounding-line Retreat of the West Antarctic Ice Sheet," *Science,* October 8, 1999.

Robert Crandall and Fred L. Smith Jr., "CO_2 Controls Are a Bad Idea, 'Voluntary' or Not," *Wall Street Journal,* July 31, 2001.

Thomas Crowley, "Causes of Climate Change over the Past 1,000 Years," *Science,* July 14, 2000.

Elizabeth Culotta, "Will Plants Profit from High CO_2?" *Science,* May 5, 1995.

David R. Easterling et al., "Climate Extremes: Observations, Modeling, and Impacts," *Science,* September 22, 2000.

Hubertus Fischer, Martin Wahlen, Jesse Smith et al., "Ice Core Records of Atmospheric CO_2 Around the Last Three Glacial Terminations," *Science,* March 12, 1999.

James K. Glassman and Sallie L. Baliunas, "Bush Is Right on Global Warming," *Weekly Standard,* June 25, 2001.

Indur M. Goklany, "Applying the Precautionary Principle to Global Warming," *Policy Study No. 158.* St. Louis, MO: Center for the Study of American Business, November 2000.

———, "Richer Is More Resilient: Dealing with Climate Change and More Urgent Environmental Problems," *Earth Report 2000,* Ronald Bailey, ed. New York: McGraw-Hill, 2000.

David Graham, "Plants: A Secret Weapon Against Global Warming?" *Technology Review,* July 1996.

Peter Gwynne, "The Cooling World," *Newsweek,* April 28, 1975.

James E. Hansen and A.A. Lacis, "Sun and Dust Versus Greenhouse Gases: An Assessment of Their Relative Roles in Global Climate Change," *Nature,* August 23, 1990.

James E. Hansen, Makiko Sato, Reto Ruedy et al., "Global Climate Data and Models: A Reconciliation," *Science,* August 14, 1998.

James W. Hurrell and Kevin E. Trenberth, "Satellite Versus Surface Estimates of Air Temperatures Since 1979," *Journal of Climate,* February 1996.

Thomas R. Karl and Richard W. Knight, "Secular Trends of Precipitation Amount, Frequency, and Intensity in the United States," *Bulletin of the American Meteorological Society,* February 1998.

Thomas R. Karl, Richard W. Knight, David R. Easterling, and Robert G. Quayle, "Indices of Climate Change for the United States," *Bulletin of the American Meteorological Society,* February 1996.

Thomas R. Karl and Kevin E. Trenberth, "The Human Impact on Climate," *Scientific American,* December 1999.

Richard A. Kerr, "Among Global Thermometers, Warming Still Wins Out," *Science,* September 25, 1998.

———, "Climate Change: Model Gets It Right—Without Fudge Factors," *Science,* May 16, 1997.

———, "Could the Sun Be Warming the Climate?" *Science,* November 1, 1991.

———, "The Right Climate for Assessment," *Science,* September 26, 1997.

W. Krabill, E. Frederick, S. Manizade et al., "Rapid Thinning of Parts of the Southern Greenland Ice Sheet," *Science,* March 5, 1999.

Judith Lean and David Rind, "The Sun and Climate," *Consequences,* Winter 1996.

Michael D. Lemonick, "Life in the Greenhouse," *Time,* April 9, 2001.

Richard S. Lindzen, "Scientists' Report Doesn't Support the Kyoto Treaty." *Wall Street Journal,* June 11, 2001.

———, "Some Coolness Concerning Global Warming," *Bulletin of the American Meteorological Society,* March 1990.

Richard S. Lindzen, Ming-Dah Chou, and Arthur Y. Hou, "Does the Earth Have an Adaptive Infrared Iris?" *Bulletin of the American Meteorological Society,* March 2001.

Alden Meyer, "Getting Their Act Together," *Nucleus,* Spring 1997.

Virginia Morell, "Are Pathogens Felling Frogs?" *Science,* April 30, 1999.

S.W. Pacala et al., "Consistent Land- and Atmosphere-Based U. S. Carbon Sink Estimates," *Science,* June 22, 2001.

Henry N. Pollack, Shaopeng Huang, and Po-Yu Shen, "Climate Change Record in Subsurface Temperatures: A Global Perspective," *Science,* October 9, 1998.

Christopher S. Potter, "Terrestrial Biomass and the Effects of Deforestation on the Global Carbon Cycle," *Bioscience,* October 1999.

S.I. Rasool and S.H. Schneider, "Atmospheric Carbon Dioxide and Aerosols: Effects of Large Increases on Global Climate," *Science,* July 9, 1972.

Paul Reiter, "From Shakespeare to Defoe: Malaria in England and the Little Ice Age," *Emerging Infectious Disease,* Centers for Disease Control and Prevention, January/February 2000.

David Rind, "Just Add Water Vapor," *Science,* August 21, 1998.

Leslie Roberts, "Global Warming: Blaming the Sun," *Science,* November 24, 1989.

"Royal Society Disputes Value of Carbon Sinks," *Nature,* July 12, 2001.

Daniel Sarewitz and Roger Pielke Jr., "Breaking the Global-Warming Gridlock," *The Atlantic Online,* July 2000.

Mark Schrope, "Consensus Science, or Consensus Politics?" *Nature,* July 12, 2001.

David Schneider, "The Rising Seas," *Scientific American,* March 1997.

Stephen H. Schneider, "The Greenhouse Effect: Science and Policy," *Science,* February 10, 1989.

Roger Sedjo, "Forest 'Sinks' as a Tool for Climate Change Policy," *Resources,* Spring 2001.

William Tucker, "The Myth of Alternative Energy," *Weekly Standard,* May 21, 2001.

P. Winsor, "Arctic Sea Ice Thickness Remained Constant During the 1990s," *Geophysical Research Letters,* March 15, 2001.

Michael Weisskopf, "Scientist Says Greenhouse Effect Is Setting In," *Washington Post,* June 24, 1988.

Dyann F. Wirth and Jacqueline Cattani, "Winning the War Against Malaria," *Technology Review,* August/September 1997.

Bernice Wuethrich, "How Climate Change Alters Rhythms of the Wild," *Science,* February 4, 2000.

Bruce Yandle, "After Kyoto: A Global Scramble for Advantage," *The Independent Review,* Summer 1999.

———, "Bootleggers, Baptists, and Global Warming," *PERC Policy Series* PS-14. Bozeman, MT: PERC, November 1998.

Internet Sites

American Wind Energy Association, September 5, 2001. www. awea.org.

Sallie Baliunas and Willie Soon, "The Sun Also Warms." Presentation at GCMOI/CEI Cooler Heads Coalition meeting, March 24, 2000. www.marshal.org.

Robert J. Bradley Jr., "Eco-Dilemmas of Renewable Energy," 1997. www.cato.org.

Climate Prediction Center (CPC), National Weather Service. www.cpc.ncep.noaa.gov.

James Hansen, Reto Ruedy, Jay Galscoe, and Makiko Sato, "Whither U.S. Climate?" NASA Goddard Institute for Space Studies, February 1, 2001. www.giss.nasa.gov.

James E. Hansen, Makiko Sato, Reto Ruedy et al., "Global Warming in the 21st Century: An Alternative Scenario," NASA Goddard Institute for Space Studies, April 17, 2001. www.giss.nasa.gov.

Craig Idso and Keith Idso, "CO_2 and Temperature: The Great Geophysical Waltz," *CO_2 Science,* April 1, 1999. http://co2 science.org.

Intergovernmental Panel on Climate Change, "Summary for Policymakers: The Scientific Basis," January 2001. www.ipcc.ch.

Intergovernmental Panel on Climate Change, "Summary for Policymakers: Climate Change 2001, Impacts, Adaptation, and Vulnerability," February 2001. www.usgcrp.gov.

David R. Legates, "Climate Models and the National Assessment." Washington, DC: George Marshall Institute. www.marshall.org.

National Geophysical Data Center, National Oceanic and Atmospheric Administration, "A Paleo Perspective on Global Warming," May 19, 2000. www.ngdc.noaa.gov.

National Oceanic and Atmospheric Administration, "Global Warming FAQs." www.ncdc.noaa.gov.

Storm Phillips, "What's Wrong with Our Weather?" www.Infoplease. com.

United Nations Development Programme, "Climate Change Information Kit," July 1999. www.undp.org.

U.S. Global Change Research Program, "Arctic Sea Ice: Changes, Causes, and Implications." Seminar, April 20, 1999. www.usgcrp.gov.

Weather Channel. www.weather.com.

Other

H. Sterling Burnett, "Cooling Overheated Global Warming Rhetoric." Brief analysis for the National Center for Policy Analysis, December 20, 2000.

John L. Daly, "The Surface Record: 'Global Mean Temperature' and How It Is Determined at Surface Level." Report prepared for the Greening Earth Society, May 2000.

Diane Douglas Dalziel, "Little Ice Age a Global Event." Position Paper. Arlington, VA: Greening Earth Society, n.d.

Robert W. Davis and David Legates, "How Reliable Are Climate Models?" Transcript of Climate Policy Briefing for Developing Country Embassies, Competitive Enterprise Institute, Washington, DC, June 5, 1998.

Energy Information Administration, Department of Energy, "What Does the Kyoto Protocol Mean to U.S. Energy Markets and the U.S. Economy?" Report prepared for the Committee on Science, U.S. House of Representatives, 1998.

Charles Keller, Tracy Light, Manvendra Dubey, and Howard Hanson, "Can Volcanically Induced Ozone Loss Resolve Discrepancies Between Surface and Tropospheric Temperature Records?" Lecture, American Geophysical Union, December 16, 1999.

David Malmquist, "Sea Level Change." Speech, May 27, 1999, Washington, DC. Sponsored by the Cooler Heads Coalition and the Competitive Enterprise Institute.

Acknowledgments

Critical Thinking About Environmental Issues: *Global Warming,* by Jane S. Shaw, is part of a series designed to bring objectivity to controversial environmental issues. Shaw, also the series editor, appreciates the support of two people who allowed her to take the time necessary to bring the broadest possible thinking and knowledge to bear on these issues. They are Terry L. Anderson, executive director of PERC—the Center for Free Market Environmentalism—in Bozeman, Montana, and Fred L. Smith Jr., president of the Competitive Enterprise Institute in Washington, D.C. She also thanks Michael Sanera for his role in initiating the series. Shaw appreciates the advice given for this volume by Robert Balling Jr., professor of climatology at Arizona State University, David Easterling, principal scientist at the National Climatic Data Center in Asheville, North Carolina, and Indur Goklany, former Julian Simon Fellow of PERC, although they are not responsible for the final contents. Shaw acknowledges the research aid of Paul Georgia, the research and writing contributions of Sara D. Ackerman, and the administrative support of Sheila Spain and Michelle Johnson at PERC.

Index

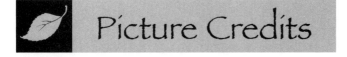

Picture Credits

Cover credit: © Photodisc
© AFP/CORBIS, 63
Associated Press, AP, 21
© Annie Griffiths Belt/CORBIS, 66
Corel Stock Photo Library, 78, 81
Jeff Di Matteo, 30
FEMA, 36
© Frank Lane Picture Agency/CORBIS, 51
Grace Fryar, 14, 15, 16, 30,
Hulton/Archive/Getty Images, 23, 34, 44, 46, 50, 64, 71, 73, 75, 77
© Wolfgang Kaehler/CORBIS, 32
Library of Congress, 17
© Joe McDonald/CORBIS, 37
National Center for Atmospheric Research/University
   Corporation for Atmospheric Research/National Science
   Foundation, 25
NOAA, 41
David Parker/Science Source/Photo Researchers, 29
© Douglas Peebles/CORBIS, 11
Photodisc, 18, 61, 80
© Roger Ressmeyer/CORBIS, 58
© Kevin Schafer/CORBIS, 57
© James A. Sugar/CORBIS, 55
© Adam Woolfitt/CORBIS, 47

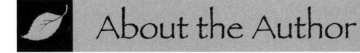

About the Author

Jane S. Shaw is a senior associate of PERC—the Center for Free Market Environmentalism—in Bozeman, Montana, a nonprofit organization that explores market solutions to environmental problems. Shaw is coauthor with Michael Sanera of *Facts, Not Fear: Teaching Children About the Environment* and coeditor with Ronald D. Utt of *A Guide to Smart Growth: Shattering Myths and Providing Solutions.* She edited *A Blueprint for Environmental Education.* Before joining PERC, Shaw was an associate economics editor of *Business Week* magazine. Before that, she worked as a reporter for McGraw-Hill Publications in New York, Washington, and Chicago. She lives in Bozeman with her husband, Richard Stroup, and their son, David.